GENUINE SCHOOL LEADERSHIP

I dedicate this book to my grandsons, Will, Luke, and Joe.
They have given new meaning to everything that I do and write.

—Ronald W. Rebore

I dedicate this book to my grandparents,
James and Virginia Evans and the late John and
late Margaret Green. They were not granted the opportunity
of a college education, but were so successful in so many ways.

—Angela L. E. Walmsley

GENUINE SCHOOL LEADERSHIP

xperience, Reflection, and Beliefs

Ronald W. Rebore • Angela L. E. Walmsley

CORWIN
PRESS
A SAGE Company

For information:

Corwin Press
A SAGE Company
2455 Teller Road
Thousand Oaks, California 91320
www.corwinpress.com

SAGE Publications Ltd.
1 Oliver's Yard
55 City Road
London, EC1Y 1SP
United Kingdom

SAGE Publications India Pvt. Ltd.
B 1/I 1 Mohan Cooperative
Industrial Area
Mathura Road, New Delhi 110 044
India

SAGE Publications Asia-Pacific
Pte. Ltd.
33 Pekin Street #02-01
Far East Square
Singapore 048763

Printed in the United States of America.

Library of Congress Cataloging-in-Publication Data
Rebore, Ronald W.
  Genuine school leadership : experience, reflection, and beliefs / by
Ronald W. Rebore and Angela L. E. Walmsley.
    p. cm.
  Includes bibliographical references and index.
  ISBN 978-1-4129-5736-6 (cloth : acid-free paper) — ISBN
978-1-4129-5737-3 (pbk. : acid-free paper)
  1. School administrators—United States. 2. Educational
leadership—United States. 3. Church and education—United States. 4. Religious
pluralism—United States. I. Walmsley, Angela Lynn Evans. II.
Title.

  LB2801.A2R435 2009
  371.2'011—dc22

                                                          2008008419

This book is printed on acid-free paper.

08 09 10 11 10 9 8 7 6 5 4 3 2 1

Acquisitions Editor: Arnis Burvikovs
Editorial Assistant: Irina Draught
Production Editor: Appingo Publishing Services
Cover Designer: Lisa Miller

Contents

Preface

This book was written because of the significant current interest in spirituality and reflection that has permeated every segment of American society including the practice of educational leadership. *Genuine School Leadership: Experience, Reflection and Beliefs* combines three of the most important components of educational leadership. In order to be reflective, an educational leader must use experience coupled with beliefs about teaching and leading others. Therefore, the authors define genuine school leadership as the ability to lead based on an individual's experience, his or her own personal beliefs (spiritual in nature), and the reflection of both. The book is divided into four major chapters. Chapter 1 presents a summary of the current notions that surround the beliefs part of genuine school leadership. In this context, indicators of spirituality in American society and culture are identified. The sources of human knowledge including scientific discoveries that impinge on spirituality are explained. The question of God and evil in the world are also treated as background to the implications of beliefs for the practice of educational leadership.

Chapter 2 presents a personal context in which genuine school leadership can be understood. Thus, the various schools of thought in psychology are identified and explained in relation to spirituality. The moral virtues of prudence, justice, fortitude, and temperance are explained in this chapter along with how human freedom enhances the quest for an authentic spirituality. Finally, the challenges of adversity, conflict, and suffering that are present in the practice of educational leadership are explored.

Chapter 3 explains how beliefs, experience, and reflection develop within the context of educational leadership. This is particularly addressed in relation to the notion of *vocations*. The authors try to demonstrate how the educational leadership profession can be viewed as a vocation. The concept of the learning community is presented as the milieu within which this vocation is carried out. Finally, the research responsibility of educational leaders is viewed as an ongoing opportunity not only to enhance the learning community but also the reflection of educational leaders.

The final chapter presents a model for the practice of educational leadership from a spiritual perspective that is termed *Transcendental Leadership*. Throughout the book the material is presented in a user-friendly manner through practical examples, case studies, and exercises. The book also includes an annotated bibliography and a significant number of references.

Acknowledgments

Ronald W. Rebore wishes to express his appreciation and gratitude to Susan Jacobsmeyer, his Graduate Assistant, for her dedicated research of the topic of spirituality and her major contribution to the Annotated Selected Bibliography.

Corwin Press gratefully acknowledges the contributions of the following individuals:

Kenneth Arndt, Superintendent
Community Unit School District #300
Carpentersville, IL

Jennifer J. Baadsgaard, Assistant Principal for Curriculum
Roosevelt High School, NEISD
San Antonio, TX

Randel Beaver, Superintendent
Archer City ISD
Archer City, TX

John Casper, Supervisor of Instruction
Nelson County Public Schools
Bardstown, KY

Gerard A. Dery, NAESP Zone 1 Director and Principal
Nessacus Regional Middle School
Dalton, MA

About the Authors

Ronald W. Rebore, Sr., PhD, is a professor at Saint Louis University located in Saint Louis, Missouri. His professional experience includes twenty-two years as an administrator: nine years as an assistant superintendent of a medium-sized suburban school district, five years as the superintendent of schools in a small suburban school district, and eight years as the superintendent of schools for a large metropolitan school district employing approximately four thousand staff members with an annual budget of approximately 170 million dollars.

Rebore has a Bachelor of Arts degree in Philosophy, a Master of Education degree in Counseling and Guidance, and a Doctor of Philosophy degree in Educational Leadership. He has taught graduate level courses in educational leadership for approximately twenty years including ethics courses. Rebore has over thirty publications; nine of which are books published by Prentice-Hall, Inc. and Allyn & Bacon. Two of the books have been published in multiple editions. The eighth edition of *Human Resources Administration in Education: A Management Approach* was released in June 2007. Two of his books have been translated into Chinese and have been adopted for use in preparing educational administrators in China.

Angela L. E. Walmsley, PhD, is an associate professor at Saint Louis University located in Saint Louis, Missouri. She has been working in the field of education for approximately thirteen years. In that time, she has taught middle school and high school mathematics both in the United States and the United Kingdom; she has taught introductory education courses, graduate level advanced education and mathematics education courses at two universities in the Saint

Louis area; and she is currently teaching statistical and educational research courses at Saint Louis University.

Walmsley has a joint Bachelor of Science degree in Mathematics and Teaching from the University of Illinois at Urbana-Champaign; a Master in Education degree in Mathematics Education and a Diploma in Statistics from the University of Dublin: Trinity College in Dublin, Ireland; and a Doctor of Philosophy degree in Curriculum and Instruction with an emphasis on Mathematics Education and Educational Research from Saint Louis University. In addition, she holds teaching certificates for the states of Illinois and Missouri, as well as Northern Ireland in the UK.

CHAPTER ONE

Understanding Experience, Reflection, and Beliefs for Educational Leadership

VIGNETTE

One day approximately one week before Halloween, some sixth grade students are sitting in their classroom waiting for the bell to ring. They begin discussing Halloween. The discussion emerges as more children participate, and the teacher eventually gets involved. Later in the day, the teacher reflects about whether she should have offered more during the conversation.

Jack: I am so bummed that we don't get to have a Halloween party and dress up now that we are in middle school. I LOVE Halloween—it's my favorite holiday.

Sophie: I really like Halloween too, especially because it's a holiday just for kids.

Jack: It's a real holiday for lots of people! My mom says that it's based around All Souls' Day in our church, and Halloween is the night that the dead come back to see the living! She says I can learn about it when I go to church and Sunday school this week.

Sophie: I never heard that. I mean, I knew it was about people dressing up and many are scary, but I didn't think it had to do with church!

Preeti: My mom is glad that we don't have to do the Halloween stuff now because she never agreed with it anyway. She always said

1

that it was a religious holiday for some, but not for us. And it wasn't fair to have it in school since we aren't supposed to have religion in school.

Sophie: Well, I think it's OK that we can have a holiday that is fun and that we all celebrate but isn't necessarily connected to a church. I mean, I guess it is for Jack, but it doesn't have to be for all of us.

Harmony: I agree with Sophie. I mean, I don't care if it's related to church or not, I just really like dressing up. But, Jack, what church do you go to where they talk about souls?

Jack: We go to St. Patrick's Church on Orange Street.

Harmony: That's really close to where I live. I go to the Fellowship Baptist Church next to our school. Preeti and Sophie, what church do you go to?

Sophie: We don't go to church. We used to go when I was little, but then my grandmother died, and my mom doesn't take us anymore.

Preeti: We don't go to a place called a church. We go to a Hindu temple to worship.

Jack: That sounds neat. What is it? I wonder how it is different.

(The teacher, overhearing the conversation, walks over to the group of students.)

Mrs. Stanton: Ok, children, the bell is going to ring soon.

Sophie: But Mrs. Stanton, we were just getting to hear about what a Hindu temple is.

Jack: Mrs. Stanton, where do you go to church?

Mrs. Stanton: Well, I'm not sure we should be talking about all our places of worship here in school.

Jack: OK, but do you believe in God? Is God different in a church than a temple?

Mrs. Stanton: My particular beliefs are personal, and I don't talk about them with students. Furthermore, I'm not comfortable talking about God in school because we really aren't supposed to.

Harmony: I don't get that. I mean, if so many of us go to church or temple or want to know more about it, why don't we get to talk about it?

Mrs. Stanton: Well, our Constitution allows us to teach children of all religions without telling them about religion in school.

Preeti: But what if we want to know more? I mean, how can I learn more about it if my teachers won't talk about it? Also, I don't mind telling someone about my temple if they will tell me about what happens at their church. I mean—we all live close to each other. How come we never get to talk about it in school even though we all go to school here?

*   *   *

The above student-driven conversation is an example of the types of situations that are presented throughout the book. As the book unfolds, the spiritual theory is explained first, followed by examples that administrators regularly deal with. In the one sample conversation above, the issue of God and existence emerges and the difference of religions is exposed (Chapter 1); the spiritual nature of the teacher is questioned (Chapter 2); a carefully answered nonbiased response is presented by the teacher and she reflects later in the day whether she should have engaged them in a real meaningful conversation (Chapter 3); and the issue of culture affecting conversation and student learning is present (Chapter 4).

THE PURPOSE FOR WRITING THIS BOOK

The purpose for writing this book is to explore the question of spirituality within the context of educational leadership and to provide practicing superintendents, principals, and other administrators with a usable clarification and understanding of *spirituality* that will help them in carrying out their responsibilities in a religiously pluralistic society. Even though the vast majority of people in the United States consider themselves to be Jewish or Christian, we are no longer just a Judeo-Christian country, but rather a Judeo-Christian-Islamic-Hindu-Buddhist-secular country. In fact, the United States is the most religiously pluralistic society in the world, which is its greatest strength. However, great attributes create great challenges and responsibilities for educational leaders. This book is also meant to provide practicing administrators with information and a plan of action that will help them view their personal spirituality as a means of enhancing their job satisfaction as an educational leader.

As a desired side effect of these objectives, it is hoped that superintendents, principals, and other administrators will be able to impart to their students a healthy pluralistic attitude that values the great spiritual diversity of our nation.

There is one more very important reason for writing this book. It might be able to contribute to the ongoing dialogue and discussion about the role that spirituality plays in the preparation of educational leaders for service in public schools.

CHAPTER OBJECTIVES

- To identify the indicators of spirituality in American society and culture
- To explore the nature of human knowledge as it relates to the issue of spirituality
- To identify the issues that surround the idea of God in relation to spirituality
- To explain the relationship between the discoveries of science and spirituality
- To explore how the problem of evil in human experience impinges on spirituality
- To explore how spirituality affects the practice of educational leadership
- To explore how spirituality impacts the formal education and preparation of educational leaders
- To explain how the profession of educational leadership can be considered a vocation

THE MILIEU

The culture of the United States takes for granted that people are spiritual by nature. Further, Americans take it for granted that most people practice their spirituality within the context of a specific religious tradition. The United States Constitution guarantees *freedom of* religion, which is a pervasive acknowledgement of the importance of religious spirituality.

What makes the discussion of spirituality difficult for some people is the notion that spirituality is a natural category of being a person. It is a way of categorizing individuals living in the United States usually through a religious tradition such as Jewish, Catholic, Baptist, Muslim, Hindu, and Buddhist. In other words it is a self-evident category that is easy to apprehend but difficult to understand. Educational leaders are required to carryout their responsibilities within this context.[1]

Contemporary Issues of Spirituality

Through the immediacy of both the electronic and print news media, the constituents of schools and school districts are constantly informed about events in all segments of local and state communities, the nation, and the world. It is this information that helps to shape public opinion about all facets of life, including spirituality and education.

The public has become acutely aware of a series of events that have taken place over the last five years, which have had a lasting effect on public attitudes. The misconduct of some church leaders, the financial misconduct of some corporate and business leaders, and the self-serving misconduct of some governmental leaders have ushered in a renewed interest in the ethical and spiritual character of our leaders and, indeed, of the moral fiber of our nation. Educational leaders are not immune from such mistrust.

Further, therapeutic cloning, the civil rights of citizens, access to medical and pharmaceutical services and products, terrorism, and equality of opportunity continue to be issues that affect millions of Americans and tens of millions of other people throughout the world. Undoubtedly, thoughtful people have confronted these issues in consort with the moral dimension of their spiritual lives.

Evidence of Spirituality Interests

Jon Meacham's new book, *The American Gospel*, has been reviewed on almost every news talk show, including Tim Russert's weekly exploration of current events. Meacham is the managing editor of *Newsweek* magazine. The premise of his book is that the founding fathers of our country were wise to embed the separation of church and state within the framework of our government. His book was prompted by the ongoing struggle to keep religious zealots from invading our public elementary and secondary schools with their brand of religion. The book speaks to an overt interest in spirituality.

Religion and spirituality are hot topics not only in the news media but also in the entertainment industry. *The Passion of Christ* and *The Da Vinci Code* are good examples of the opinions that seem to continually bombard the public. The real issue, of course, is the intense interest in spirituality that flourishes outside the confines of churches.

The *Chronicle of Higher Education* reported in the January 7, 2005, issue: "Announce a course with 'religion' in the title, and you will have an overflow population." The March 10, 2006, issue declared that "8 out of 10 academics say they are spiritual, and 64% call themselves religious." A most interesting indicator appeared on the cover of the October 25, 2004, issue of *Time* magazine that carried the caricature of a woman praying or meditating with the caption, "The God Gene."

A rather significant indication of the importance of spirituality in the contemporary milieu is the recently released preliminary report of the Task Force on General Education of Harvard's Faculty of Arts and Sciences. It sets the stage for revising the core curriculum of the College, which would be implemented through courses that are required of all Harvard's undergraduates. The report observes that religion is a reality of life in the twenty-first century and, as such, impacts perceptions on issues in science, medicine, law, culture, and economics. Thus the report sets forth a core curriculum requirement dealing with *reason and faith* in order for students to understand the relationship between religion and secular ideas, institutions, and practices.

This revised approach did not get final approval, but the observation of the report that students should be encouraged to become more self conscious about the religious beliefs of others and themselves is revolutionary at a secular university.[2]

Another interesting project that clearly reflects the intense interest of the American people in the spiritual dimension of life is the *Programs for the Theological Exploration of Vocation*. This is a project of the Lilly Endowment, Inc. that was initiated in 1999 through an invitation to a selected group of colleges and universities asking them to develop or strengthen existing programs that deal with vocation. Specifically, the call was for programs that would assist students in examining their understanding of the relationship between faith and vocational choice, and to create opportunities for students to reflect on a call to ministry. Finally, the invitation encompassed the development of programs that would equip faculty and staff to teach and mentor students in the area of vocational choice informed by each student's faith.

In 2000 the Lilly Endowment granted approximately forty million dollars to twenty colleges and universities for the exploration of vocations. In 2001 an additional twenty-nine colleges and universities were awarded approximately fifty-seven million dollars; and in 2002 an additional thirty-nine colleges and universities were granted approximately seventy-nine million dollars. Thus a total of eighty-eight institutions of higher education received approximately one hundred and seventy-six million dollars to help students explore the link between faith and vocation.[3]

An Explanation of Terms

Just from this brief introduction, it is easy to see that much confusion can arise about terms that are commonly used to indicate the more ethereal dimension of the human phenomenon. The term *spirituality* and the other four terms set forth in this section are particularly difficult to understand in relation to spirituality and to each other. Also, the common approach to the process of defining terms does not truly give justice to the complexity of the terms; thus what follows is more of a description than a definition.

Spirituality

A necessary characteristic of being human is change. No one stays the same. That change can be either beneficial or detrimental. If it is beneficial, it is commonly referred to as growing and developing. If it is detrimental, it is commonly referred to as regressing.

Thus the first given about spirituality is that it must be evolutionary in the sense that a person grows and develops throughout the various stages of life.

Second, growing and developing does not come easily. It requires continual decision making concerning those options in life that contribute to growth and development. Personal freedom to make such choices is the fundamental ability to living as a spiritual person. In order to exercise such freedom, a person must have an interior life of reflection that leads to self-knowledge and understanding.

Third, often contrary to common parlance, self-knowledge and understanding can be correctly revealed to a person through only his or her relationships to other people. Further, a person cannot fashion those relationships as the *stance of an observer*, but rather must be an engaged person in the various communities to which he or she belongs and with individual people.

Finally, a person's growth and development through the exercise of freedom that leads to self-knowledge and understanding in community with others must eventuate in a life filled with purpose, which focuses on the welfare of others.

The process of gaining self-knowledge and understanding and making decisions arises from the sources through which we gain access to the raw material of self and decision making. In a spiritual context those sources are ontological, experiential, and faith-based insights. These three sources will be explained in the section on *Human Insights and Spirituality.*

Ethics

There are many similarities between spirituality and ethics such as the need to be self-reflective, to freely exercise judgment, and to be engaged with other people. However, the realm of ethics deals with making decisions about the most honorable course of action that a person should take in a given dilemma through the use of reason, which is a dimension of experiential insight. In other words, ethical actions are right conduct for the welfare of other people as individuals or for those belonging to a particular community. Thus the right of teachers to a procedural due process through a performance evaluation procedure is an ethical responsibility of a principal or superintendent depending on the organizational structure of a school district.

Religiosity

Most people practice their spirituality through a particular religious tradition. Even though they still have ontological, experiential, and faith-based insights, they prefer to base their self-reflection, decision making, and engagement with other people through the tenets of doctrine and morality set forth in the religious tradition to which they belong.

Ideology

This is a particularly interesting phenomenon. Ideology is usually conceived of as a political strategy to accomplish a particular goal in the life of a community. The founders of our country brandished an ideology that was revolutionary at the time because it recognized the rights of the individual to life, liberty, and the pursuit of happiness. Through a constitutional government, each citizen has the right to participate in the governmental decision-making process either by running for political office or by voting for those who represent him or her in government service.

Vocation

Educational leaders are public figures in the sense that they provide a public service, which is highly visible to all members of the community they serve. Further, the service that educational leaders and teachers provide requires parents to entrust their children to the care and education of those leaders. Because children are so vulnerable and because the caring and education of children is so personal, the manner in which superintendents, principals, and other educational leaders perceive their responsibilities is an important factor in the wellbeing of children.

The word *vocation* emanates from the Latin word, *vocare*, which means to be called as in an invitation or summons. Educational leaders are contracted by boards of education who are the elected representatives of the taxpayers in the community they serve.

Superintendents, principals, and other educational leaders are paid with tax money. Thus in a real sense educational leaders have been invited and summoned to be of service to all members of the community through the care and education of the children living in the community they serve.

Of course, children are the next generation of Americans who will have the responsibility of caring for, protecting, and leading not only the current generation but also the generation that will come after them. Thus the economic, social, physical, psychological, and spiritual welfare of current and future generations depends on the quality of care and education that the current generation of children receives. Obviously, this is the intergenerational stewardship responsibility of educational leaders, which is why educational leadership is a vocation.

Synthesis

Obviously, there are elements of each term present in each other term. However, for this presentation the predominant themes in the *spirituality* and *vocation* explanations constitute the perspectives that are used throughout this book. The authors recognize the human ability and freedom to reformulate the explanations and to find new ways of distinguishing or not distinguishing the content of the terms. However, they are constructs that help the authors to focus on how spirituality informs the practice of educational leadership.

Practical Discussions and Examples

Every educational leader is spiritual. It is an innate quality. However, not every educator is religious. While many educators are religious, those who work in public school are often afraid to even mention the word religion or spirituality for fear of public uproar about the separation between "church and state." Some very religious leaders choose to work in a school of that particular religion so that they can also teach those ideals as part of their vocation.

Most administrators (and teachers) choose education as their profession because they have an innate feeling or drive to help others.

They may enjoy working with children, but they ultimately choose education because they see a societal need to work in a helping profession where they can influence and teach children in a positive way. Therefore, the choice of vocation is based in a spiritual calling that is not necessarily religious. Of course, there are religious educators who have a calling to teach in a particular religion, but there are also teachers who are not religious, but consider themselves spiritual. That is, they see a calling where they can cause change and hopefully improve society by choosing teaching and leadership as a vocation.

How can an educational leader be religious or spiritual and effectively lead a school filled with a diverse range of children from many religious backgrounds? How can this leader do so without "stepping on toes" of various religious groups and at the same time be impartial to his or her personal religion or spirituality? How can a teacher address the questions her students have about a T-shirt a student is wearing that day in school that says, "In the event of nuclear war, the ban on school prayer will be lifted"? I imagine that prayer in school was inevitable for many of the students and teachers at the Columbine school shooting, and I also imagine that few people were thinking about a controversial prayer T-shirt at the time. Should a teacher be concerned when a parent sends an e-mail to her at school and signs it, "Love in Jesus' name"?

As mentioned previously, there are many atrocities occurring in the United States, our schools, and the world today. Likewise, there are many deeply religious people in our world today who want to spread their news about faith and spirituality. How can teachers and students make sense of these without some moral or ethical direction from the school administrator? Every person has a spiritual component to his or her makeup. It is in what *way* administrators use spiritual leadership that can positively or negatively affect the leadership of the school.

Practically, this may include providing examples of when religious discussion goes "too far" in the classroom. An administrator will no doubt be called upon from various parents about concerns of celebration in December in classrooms. Is an administrator effective in setting rules about such issues, or should the community help decide? These are the types of issues that will be addressed in the practical examples and discussions throughout the book.

Human Insights

There are three sources of insight that all humans have and utilize throughout their lives. Further, all people have the capability of reflecting on the spiritual dimension of the human phenomenon through these sources. A realistic understanding of spirituality demands that educational leaders appreciate the sources of human insight that provide the foundation for making personal and professional decisions.

Ontological Insight

This type of insight is predicated on *what* and *who* people are because they exist. It is the realm of insight generated through physical apprehension and experiences as feelings, emotions, instinct, and reason. It is the milieu of immediate self-knowledge that is self-evident. The term *ontological* comes from the Greek word for being, *ontos*. The implication is that humans have such insight because they are who they are. Thus a person knows instinctively the emotions of love, fear, and happiness in addition to all other emotions and combinations of emotions.

A female knows instinctively what it means to be a female and needs no tutoring in that area. A father immediately understands what it means to be a father when his wife gives birth. A person understands the physical effects of illness without explanations, which is the reason why physicians question patients about their self-apprehension of what is wrong with them.

This type of insight is the most primitive and fundamental of all self knowledge. The prominent psychologist Carl Jung identified this receptacle as the psyche where the *collective unconscious* resides. He thought that human evolution produced a residue that all people have inherited and which influences their perception of life experiences such as the reaction to authority figures. It is also the receptacle of subconscious residue that has been generated by our individual past experiences, especially in childhood. These subconscious emotions influence our daily activities. However, most contemporary psychologists would state that these influences do not predetermine our decision making, because humans are capable of overcoming all influences.

The way people empathize with others is through projecting their learned ontological feelings and emotions onto them. Empathy occurs through analogy. The other is a person and thus he or she must know what it means to love someone or to be afraid because each person understands such emotions from his or her ontological insight.

Experiential Insight

Experience is what a person acquires through external stimuli, which includes both formal and informal education. As a human being, a person learns something through every poem, movie, work of art, music composition, conversation, injury, and so forth that he or she encounters. It is the very act of living life.

Of course, it is the reason why people with a certain amount of experience are the most desired candidates for some jobs. Older people are venerated in some cultures because of their life experiences. The assumption is that they know more and understand more about how to live life in a better way.

Faith-Based Insight

There is a gap between what we know from ontological and experiential insights that can be filled only through faith. Faith is what we believe that cannot be proven through reason or experience. We believe just because we choose to believe. Most of what we believe is predicated on the human authority of our parents or religious leaders. Other beliefs are accepted because they are contained in documents that people consider to have emanated through divine inspiration such as the Bible or Koran (or Qur'an), or that have a symbolic meaning that represents a spiritual truth such as the Declaration of Independence.

Synthesis

Obviously, the daily life activities of people are not divided into these discrete types of insight. Rather, they inform each other.

It is just as correct to state that ontological insight is informed by experience and faith, or that experience is informed by ontological and faith insights, or that faith is informed by ontological and experiential insights. Humans are integrated and holistic beings who utilize all these insights as they make personal and professional decisions.

Practical Discussions and Examples

In understanding the human insights about spirituality, administrators must be aware of the three main insights that make up each individual person. Every teacher, student, and parent comes to the school with innate experiences, with learned experiences, and with faith. An administrator must be aware that all three of these comprise an individual; therefore, focusing on only one will not educate the child fully. For example, in leading the school as a safe place for all students, the principal asks students, parents, and teachers to have faith that the school will remain safe (faith knowledge). These individuals often respect and believe authority figures; therefore, they do not continually question the safety of the school (ontological knowledge). However, the principal must educate the parents, students, and teachers on some aspects of safety in order to maintain a safe environment (experiential knowledge). An administrator who possesses only one or two of these forms of knowledge in a situation will have a difficult time in leading the school. As explained previously, these forms of knowledge do not operate separately but together to form the beliefs of a person. Therefore, a leader must provide information when necessary and ask for belief in himself or herself when necessary. Of course, faith in a school leader is often compromised when the leader's actions do not warrant respect or faith from parents, teachers, or the community. Furthermore, ontological knowledge and faith will work only part of the time…much of what parents, teachers, and students need is experiential knowledge. Likewise, administrators need to have faith in what they are doing, but they also need the knowledge, skills, and dispositions to effectively lead a school by making informed and evidence-based decisions.

THE PERSPECTIVE OF INQUIRY

World View

From human consciousness emanates the context within which spiritual norms are identified. Essentially, consciousness consists of thought, reflection, and liberty. These components are operationalized through human experience, understanding, and judgment. Thus, spiritual norms emerge. The evolutionary perspective and other scientific knowledge have created a new worldview and vision that compels humanity to reevaluate previous spiritual norms.

The classical worldview considers the world as a finished product and holds that the experiences of people will allow them to grasp a clear understanding of reality. People, therefore, can have a high degree of certitude about spiritual principles that will remain forever valid. The only path to right conduct is formulated using universal principles in a deductive method, which will yield secure and complete conclusions. People with this perspective emphasize the importance of adhering to preestablished norms and complying with authority. Superintendents and principals agreeing with this worldview will probably find it difficult to accept unconventional values.

The evolutionary worldview sets forth that the world is dynamic and evolving; progress and change are its hallmarks. The experiences of people allow them to identify individual traits within concrete and historical particulars. Thus, the path to right conduct is primarily through induction from particular experiences. Some conclusions may change with an increase in knowledge. Thus, incompleteness and error are possible, which could lead to a revision of principles. Adaptation to change and responsibility are characteristic of this worldview.[4] Superintendents and principals following this perspective probably would be more accepting of unconventional values.

Of course, most people would agree that the prudent approach to developing spiritual norms lies somewhere in the middle of these two divergent positions. Therefore, superintendents and principals should use kindness and understanding when dealing with people who do things that they consider inappropriate or wrong because circumstances could have diminished their culpability.

Critical Reflection on Spirituality

Critical reflection takes into account the importance of practice as the phenomenon upon which theory and spiritual values are based. Everything begins with practice. Knowing and understanding what is occurring in schools and school districts is the only way to evaluate effective leadership. Leadership cannot be a top-down phenomenon, but rather must begin with what is taking place in the classrooms, corridors, cafeteria, media center, parking lots, and playgrounds. It also means knowing what is going on with the physical systems in the facilities. Finally, it means knowing and understanding the attitudes, emotions, and opinions of all stakeholders. Parents, students, teachers, staff members, administrators, and the public at large reflect in their daily lives the values, accomplishments, issues, and problems of public education and the educational practices of particular schools and school districts.

It is from this base that school administrators can ascertain if what they believe in terms of educational theory really works. Does block scheduling work? How successful is teacher empowerment as a management strategy? What about the effectiveness of helping students develop critical thinking skills? The common mistake that many superintendents and principals are guilty of in relation to school reform is making decisions by fiat. There is no question about the value and importance of educational theory. Practice without theory is chaos. Some superintendents and principals move from one new approach to another just in the hope that something new will work better than what is currently being tried. This is a regular occurrence in some schools and school districts particularly where good intentioned but ill informed noneducational reformers with influence and an agenda can capture the attention of school board members.

All theory is predicated on a system of spiritual norms. Teacher empowerment is based on the assumption that professional educators are skilled and dedicated professionals who are capable of making their own decisions not only about their classrooms and disciplines but also about what works best in education. At the school and school district level, this means sharing the leadership responsibility with teachers and staff members. Thus theory without spiritual values is also chaos. Not making the connection that theory is founded on spiritual values is the same problem that arises when practice is not viewed as emanating from theory.

There is another important aspect to the decision-making paradigm. There is a reciprocal relationship between practice, theory, and spiritual values. Not only does everything begin with practice but in fact, practice can change theory which, in turn, can change a superintendent's and principal's spiritual values. Such a change in spiritual values can further alter a person's theory which will ultimately affect practice

For purposes of discussion, practice can be considered the first level of reflection, theory the second level of reflection, and spiritual values the third level. This is a rather easy paradigm to understand but can be a difficult one to implement because reflection takes time and energy. Reflection requires a superintendent or principal to hesitate before making commitments and decisions. That is often very difficult to do when conflicts occur. However, it is more important that the mechanics of reflection constitute the disposition of superintendents and principals; thereby, influencing them to search for the relationship between practice, theory, and spiritual values.

This search, of course, takes self-knowledge and commitment. It begs the question, "How can I make sure my practice, theory of leadership, and spiritual values match up?" It further requires a superintendent or principal to bring these three elements into synchronization, which in some instances could bring discontent on the part of faculty and staff. A principal who believes that he or she needs to empower his or her faculty to take more leadership responsibility for the instructional program may find a certain degree of resistance because the faculty might view such a position as encroaching on their already overcrowded schedules.[5]

Practical Discussions and Examples

A leader cannot be effective without the use of ethical norms that occur in his or her school district. Ethical norms are what provide the background information that a school leader uses to make decisions. However, stagnant ethical norms will not provide a leader with the information and tools that he or she will need. Thus, the leader must use the reflection paradigm constantly to perfect and evolve his or her leadership skills and decisions. An effective leader is one who makes decisions based on evidence and input from appropriate stakeholders, staff, and students. These ethical norms are sometimes already established in a school because of previously made decisions influenced by these same groups. As with any leadership position, an administrator must constantly change as needed. Making ethical decisions can be difficult when religion is part of the issue.

For example, suppose that Mrs. Graham is a new principal in a small rural, southern community. This community is traditionally Baptist and is accustomed to influencing members within the community by regular discussion of God and the Bible. Upon Mrs. Graham's appointment to the school, she realizes that this high school has a regularly held Bible study group during a study hall period of the day. This has been the cultural norm of the school for many years. However, after she arrives, a small group of parents approach her about their concern for religion during the school day. They state that they held the same concern previously, but that the previous principal approved of the Bible study group during school hours so they did not question it further. Mrs. Graham discusses the issue with the superintendent and the school legal counsel since she has her doubts that this should be occurring during the school day. But because the school is so much a part of the community, she realizes that completely eliminating the group could cause friction between members of the community and herself as a new leader in the school district and community. Therefore, after discussion with other administrators, parents, students, and some community leaders, she decides that the school will still allow a Bible study group but that it has to be outside of regularly scheduled school hours so that there is no question that religion is being "taught" during the school day.

Mrs. Graham has taken a very delicate issue and changed the norm without eliminating it completely. Therefore, she used evidence provided by those around her to inform her decision and make some changes. She may have her own religious beliefs; however, her decision is based mainly on beliefs about what the curriculum in her public school should contain. Her philosophical values as an educator surpassed her personal spiritual or religious influence. These are the types of reflections and decisions that educational leaders must constantly make which in turn cause change in theory and practice.

THE QUESTION OF GOD

The Western Tradition

Because of litigation over the separation of church and state, educational administrators are reluctant to talk about God. Yet, the idea of God is always lingering in the back regions of human consciousness. Another reason for this reluctance is usually the heightened fear of offending the sensibilities of other individuals or groups. In addition, there is significant constitutional and legal precedence protecting freedom of religion to a degree where it is better to say and do nothing that might be construed as promoting either religion or atheism. Of course, along this belief/unbelief continuum lie multiple intervals; in fact, there are some schools and school districts in the United States that are virtually religious because a majority of the student body and community are members of a specific religious tradition.

Further, administrators and teachers are engaged in a deliberative activity, molding and forming the moral character and attitudes of children and young adults, to such an extent that it is almost impossible for the educators to suspend their religious belief systems when interacting with students. The word "God" may never be spoken in these encounters, but many educators, students, and parents are certainly aware of the source from which their rules and norms have been borrowed. There is a tacit understanding. Thus not to include a treatment on the idea of belief in God in a book on spirituality would certainly beg the question.

The idea of God's existence has been and continues to be an extremely complex but fascinating issue. Every mature person has thought about this issue at some point in his or her life. It is an issue that challenges not only human intelligence but also human emotions, because the notion of God has such a profound effect on how people understand the purpose of existence in this world.

It is important for educational administrators to know the deist arguments for the existence of God, which predate and support the current debate concerning the intelligent design argument. It is not presented here in advocacy for belief in God, but rather for the educational benefit of administrators since they are constantly encountering people who promote a deistic spirituality. Many arguments for the existence of God have appeared during certain periods of history and have been employed with varying degrees of success. These arguments have been categorized by scholars according to the fundamental elements that distinguish one argument from another.

One of the oldest is the ideological argument, of which there are many versions. Gottfried Leibniz defended the ideological approach and used it to formulate his unique perspective on the God question as follows: Because eternal truths are principles that regulate all existence, they must preexist in a necessary substance from which all truth is derived.[6]

A second category of arguments starts with the proposition that the idea of God is that of which no greater idea can be conceived. If such a being had a reality only in thought, a person could then conceive of a greater being, a being which exists in objective reality. Thus, the idea of God as absolute perfection must be the idea of an existing being and, therefore, a person cannot have the ideal of God and deny the existence of God at the same time.[7]

René Descartes (1596–1650) is perhaps the most famous modern philosopher to attempt an argumentation for the existence of God. Descartes' argument centered on the truth of ideas: Everything of which a person has a clear and distinct idea is true; and whatever is true is real because a person cannot have an idea of pure negation.[8]

Classical Logic and the Question of God

Writing in the field of theodicy, Bernardino Bonansea, simplified the various arguments for the existence of God by preserving key elements while disregarding those elements that he considered no longer relevant because of scientific advances. His argument is as follows:

Something exists. This is an affirmation of every person's intimate knowledge that he or she exists. It is a self-evident truth immediately derived from the personal experience of each person. Thus, it needs no demonstration.

If something exists, something has always existed. The ancient and often-quoted dictum, *ex nihilo nihil fit* (from nothing, nothing comes), sets forth the essence of this assertion. Thus, if at any moment in the past, nothing existed, nothing would exist today.

If something has always existed, it exists through its own power. Existence is an act that is simple in the sense that it cannot be a process whereby there is a gradual development from nothing into being. A process involves a series of acts or operations in something that already exists which leads to an end or a change in something. Between nothing and existence, there is no transitional development; there is an absolute gap between nothing and existence. Thus, when people speak of a work of art being brought into existence, obviously what is meant is that there has been a change in materials already existing.

If other beings exist, a first self-existent being is both necessary and eternal. This is the central point of the argument for the existence of God. A being which depends on another being for its existence cannot be fully explained or understood except by its relation to a necessary being.

A self-existent being is the cause of all other beings. A self-existent being must be infinitely perfect because neither it nor contingent beings can place limitations on a necessary being.[9] Of itself, this exercise in logic does not directly prove the existence of God, but taps into a common thought process.

Intelligent Design and the Question of God

The question of God takes on an entirely different perspective with the advent of intelligent design, which is a theory that accepts scientific information and discoveries in physics, biology, astronomy, geology, and other scientific disciplines with one exception.

The exception is the belief that there is a God who is the creator of the universe and everything in it, including human beings. Further, all creation has occurred and will continue to unfold through a long process that some people view as purposeful evolution. Obviously, from the term itself, intelligent design includes the notions of intentionality and purpose by a supreme designer that permeates all creation. Intelligent design is a new wrinkle in an old debate that had flourished in the Scopes monkey trial in the 1920s and in recent bouts with the Creation Science movement.

The traditional understanding of evolution is governed by the principle of *natural selection*. This is the tediously long process of solving problems in the natural world and, particularly in biology, of discarding and adapting in order to solve particular problems. The emphasis is on the past and present, not the future. Thus Darwinian evolutionists see a design in the natural world through natural selection that allows life to continue through change and adaptation. For example, human beings are still evolving through reproduction, which alters the genetic make-up of entire populations through the natural selectivity of people. Diseases that once devastated entire populations are now mitigated through our naturally evolved immune system. However, the fear of catastrophic disease that was once under control can be a very real danger because the gene pool has been evolving and may have lost a certain type of immunity.

Related to this research on evolution is the research that is being conducted on a genetic connection to the notion of God. Researchers are trying to demonstrate that there is a need for belief in God. Most researchers begin with the common understanding that the idea of a single deity or multiple deities is a common occurrence in almost all human cultures regardless of their geographical isolation.

Once again the exercise of intelligent design principles will not directly prove the existence of a grand designer, God. Rather, it must be relegated to the faith of believers.[10]

Practical Discussions and Examples

The issue of God is an important one for educational leaders because of the many influences in our country and in our students who believe in God. In particular, when one studies "World Religions," it becomes apparent that almost every religion believes in a form of God or of a "larger than life" spiritual being. Therefore, many of the students and teachers that an administrator will work with may have an idea of a God in his or her life. There is the everlasting debate about the mottoes "In God we trust" and "One nation, under God" that continues to surface in the media and in our court system. Educational leaders must deal with these issues on school grounds and in the lives of a variety of families.

Our school systems exist based on two things: tradition and written law or documentation. The schools in the United States have a long tradition of religious influence without the teaching of religion in schools. Furthermore, students come to school with spirituality, ethics, and morals from their families; many times they are not common. Therefore, the educational leader is responsible for leading a community that has its own cultural norms that are based in the various families and the community surrounding it. However, educational leaders must try to abide by law regulating schools, and for many this involves the issue of "church and state."

For example, in one small community in Illinois, it has been tradition that the high school has what they call a *baccalaureate*. In this community, a baccalaureate is basically a religious service for high school graduating seniors, and it is often conducted around the time of formal graduation. Therefore, the graduating class wears their formal regalia of caps and gowns to attend this service which is held on school property in the gymnasium where graduation is held a few days later. As an administrator, the principal must decide how to keep this tradition that the community and graduates want, but still withstand guidelines of the separation of "church and state." Therefore, this service has evolved over time to include only those graduates and families who want to attend; it is always held in the evening after the school day, and the speaker is a religious leader in the community who is voted on by the graduates. The speaker is given guidelines not to profess a particular faith, but to provide a moral, ethical, and uplifting speech for the graduates as they leave high school and make the transition to their next stage of life. What has evolved is a community united in spirit without a particular religion. The message includes values of the community for young adults in a positive way.

This example describes a situation in which an educational leader must deal with the issues of God and religion in a setting that benefits the community. The educator must be aware of how many people have God in their lives, and how important messages can be professed without teaching about God.

NEUROSCIENCE RESEARCH

An area of interest in the field of neurobiology centers on the phenomenon of consciousness. Further, the major issue of inquiry is concerned with the possible demonstration that consciousness has an immaterial aspect rather than being the product of brain activation patterns. The Templeton Foundation will contribute approximately thirty-five million dollars during the next year to fund research in the area of science and religion that deals with materialism in neurobiology.

Researchers at the University of Pennsylvania Center for Spirituality and the Mind have been using brain scanning to detect the changes in the brains of Buddhist nuns and other meditators during spiritual exercises. The results indicate that there are physiological changes that occur during the exercises. The Center draws upon other research from the fields of bioethics, medicine, neuroscience, and religious studies.

A fascinating area of research at the University of California at Los Angeles involves the treatment of people with obsessive-compulsive disorders. A research professor of psychiatry utilizes a focused-attention therapy that has altered the behavior of the patients' brains. This research tries to demonstrate that such changes in the brain could not occur if the mind emerges solely from brain activity. In other words, the researchers are trying to assert that the mind can exercise control over the brain and thus exists separate from the body.

Tibetan Buddhists have become willing participants in this type of research. In fact, the Dalai Lama has been attending a series of meetings with neurobiologists since the 1980s on the physiological effects of meditation. Researchers at Harvard, Princeton, and the Universities of California at Davis and at Los Angeles are also separately conducting studies on meditation. Certain aspects of this research deal with how meditation can help students even at the elementary school level.[11]

Appendix A contains additional information about science and spirituality, which centers on recent discoveries in astronomy, physics, and geology. The reason why it is not included in this chapter and placed in an appendix is that it is detailed and might distract from the flow of presentation in the main body of the chapter. However, it is important to understand that natural science researchers along with researchers in the humanities and social sciences are engaged in the question of spirituality. It adds texture to the context of this inquiry, and it is the environment within which educational leaders are engaged along with faculty members in curricular and program development.

Practical Discussions and Examples

Scientific research and the issue of spirituality can sometimes be a very controversial one. Most likely an educational leader will at some point have to deal with community leaders or parents who have issues with the science curriculum. There has been continual debate over the topics of evolution, creation, and intelligent design. In fact, many people believe that intelligent design is a type of creationism thought and that it is in stark contrast to evolution, which is most often part of a science curriculum. In fact, evolution may leave space for an "intelligent designer" in its theories; therefore, some feel that intelligent design should possibly be part of a curriculum as well. Despite what religious or science theories or background an administrator has or believes, there is a likely chance that an educational administrator will have to have this discussion with board members, teachers, and parents. In dealing with this issue, an administrator should again look at tradition and law to balance a decision or conversation about what should or should not be taught in the classroom. An administrator may likely have his or her own opinion about creation of the Earth and human beings, but again the administrator must leave out his personal beliefs and take those values that he or she must use in making decisions for the school community.

THE PROBLEM OF EVIL

The sexual abuse of students by teachers and other school personnel is perhaps the most emotion-laden issue confronting educational administrators. Obviously, the reason why this is so difficult to understand lies in the fact that adults, who have been entrusted with the care of certain children, manipulate and use them for their own personal gratification. In a more subtle way is the harm that students endure at the hands of incompetent teachers and administrators. It is difficult to measure the full impact that such individuals have had on the learning instructional process, but it is safe to say that some students have experienced gaps in their learning.

On a much broader scale, entire nations and certain ethnic groups have been abused and subjugated by unscrupulous people. Dominant cultures, politics, and economics have always allied to marginalize significant numbers of people. The examples of this and other types of evil are legion.

Throughout the centuries, the problem of evil has occupied the minds not only of theologians and philosophers but also poets, artists, novelists, and dramatists as well as educators and scientists.[12]

Moral and Physical Evil[13]

Augustine (354–430) was one of the primary authors responsible for enlightening the people of his time about moral evil. He thought that moral evil was always initiated by people who are greedy, conceited, cruel, raged, contemptuous, and so on. In other words, human beings have always been and will continue to be their own worst enemies. The people who produce evil, according to Augustine, have misused their own free will.

Humans have not only been guilty of horrendous evil toward their own kind; they have also been extraordinarily callous in regard to animal life and the environment. David Hume extended the list of evils to include those that are perpetrated by people against themselves—shame, rage, anxiety, fear, and despair.

Equally horrendous physical evils have continually befallen the human race. Disease, hunger, and malnutrition are difficult to ponder and evoke terrible images of suffering. Acts of God such as floods, hurricanes, tornadoes, and volcanoes cause immense suffering. The physical effects of fire destroy animal habitats and property, and leave people maimed and mutilated.

Various Solutions to the Problem of Evil[14]

Basically there are two dimensions to the problem of evil. The first dimension is usually referred to as the *existential dimension* because it focuses on the daily struggle of people to cope with their personal sufferings. The second is usually referred to as the *theoretical dimension* because it focuses on the formulation of rationale solutions to the problem of evil. For most people, the existential dimension is the most important because it is the most urgent. When faced with suffering and anguish, people generally do not have the emotional stability necessary to search for ultimate answers.

There are a number of techniques which people use to cope with their suffering: renunciation of the world and seeking mystical knowledge through various forms of meditation, religious ritual and worship; performing acts of charity toward others; and making sacrifices for the welfare of others.

Philosophers have written extensively about the power of persons to cause evil in the world. All entities have some degree of creativity; thus, there arises some risk of conflict and suffering. The philosopher John Hick used the writings of Irenaeus, a theologian in the third century, as the grounding for his spirituality. Hick argues for two stages of creation. The first stage occurred over a long evolutionary period during which humans developed their physical nature; the second stage is the present period during which individuals have the opportunity to develop their spiritual nature. The issue of personal freedom is key to this position.

Conclusions

The first conclusion is that moral evil is the result of human beings abusing their freedom. The second is that physical evil is a side effect of the laws of nature, which are necessary to support human life. Finally, there is immense good in the world that sustains most people. The awesome beauty of nature and the engulfing sense of happiness that comes from loving and being loved validate the trust that most people have in a spirituality, which flourishes beyond human understanding.[15]

Practical Discussions and Examples

The problems of evil are issues that administrators will need to deal with regularly in leadership positions. Evil and moral wrong-doings occur on many levels, ultimately when a particular individual or authority figure with power makes wrong choices. This can happen in a school where a teacher feels superior to his or her students and belittles students at every opportunity. Unfortunately, there are too many of these teachers still in classrooms—in fact, many state that they are just "hanging around to retire." Nevertheless, students who are constantly belittled either in front of others or as a group are experiencing negative effects of the learning environment. An educational leader will be involved in helping to monitor this behavior and stopping it, if possible, when it is happening in his or her school. On the other end of the spectrum, an administrator may have to deal with a teacher who is found guilty of sexual misconduct with a student. Again, a teacher has chosen the wrong path and evil is leading his or her actions with the students. Administrators are part of all of these conversations and situations.

On another level, an administrator must also constantly reflect and evaluate that he or she is not tempted by evil. Many administrators feel they are in positions of power over teachers, parents, and students. An administrator must constantly make sure that he or she is making ethical decisions at all times. Free will is the spiritual concept that all individuals are given the opportunities to make decisions, and each individual can make a good or bad decision at any given time. Those who make bad decisions have wrongly used their free will and are contributors to evil. A successful administrator continues to use free will for the good of the school and children—not for personal gain.

A different aspect of evil is that which is grounded in religion. Many religious people have issues of faith and negative images of God when something evil happens around them or in their lives. For example, students who experience a school shooting are experiencing evil around them. A student whose parent dies unexpectedly in a car accident feels that God is evil for allowing such a thing to happen. Those students, and teachers, will have these types of issues and will need to deal with them in some way. This often happens in the school setting. If a student is killed, the other students are affected in such a way that conversations need to take place in order to help them cope and heal. Sometimes these conversations include God or religion—often initiated by the student. Support staff, such as counselors or psychologists who are brought into school to help in a mass situation like this, must be prepared to have discussions about religion, God, an afterlife, reasons for evil, ways to cope with evil, and ways to prevent evil. An administrator must also be prepared for dealing with these types of evils and the issue of God and religion that become topics in schools at times like these. Administrators must not lose sight of the purpose of school: to fully educate children. If it involves the discussion of evil in light of select religious issues at select times with particular students, then it should be embraced and not avoided.

Practical Discussions and Examples

In the world today, there are many issues that students, teachers, and, hence, administrators deal with on a regular basis. For so long, educators have tried to separate "church and state" by leaving religion and spirituality out of schools. A turning point for Americans, regardless of religion or school, was the September 11, 2001, attack on the World Trade Center. It was at this point that many educators and leaders felt that there was something wrong with the moral fiber of our country. Many of the men who were part of that attack partook in it in the name of religion. How could students understand that idea when our schools won't talk about spirituality or religion? Since that time, some leaders have felt that instead of shying away from spirituality, maybe we should embrace it and learn from each other. An analogy of this is the issue of race in our country. For so long, different races did not embrace diversity or talk about diversity. Many schools now are very diverse with a large number of different ethnicities and races. An educational leader who can lead his school to embrace those diversities can do the same thing in relation to spirituality.

However, this will be new ground for many schools and administrators. The separation between church and state has helped aid this country by preventing religious organizations or cults from forcing their one religion or belief system on a group of students. Therefore, administrators must monitor that teachers and leaders in their school district and schools use spirituality as a discussion tool rather than for "brainwashing" or convincing.

Furthermore, administrators must acknowledge their own spirituality and how it affects their leadership. Does it make them stronger leaders? Every person has free will, makes choices, and must face consequences in light of those decisions. Each administrator must use the reflection paradigm to constantly evaluate decisions based on the ethical norms of the community, school, and the United States. An administrator must make decisions and be a role model for students and staff in a community. Therefore, a self-reflection on personal spirituality and how spirituality affects schools is appropriate for all school leaders.

SUMMARY

This chapter began with a look at human insights and spirituality— stressing the importance of spirituality in people's lives as is seen by current media. Furthermore, some definitions of important terms related to spirituality were provided in order to understand and talk about spirituality, religion, and vocation as it pertains to an educational leader's life. Next, the human insights relating to spirituality were discussed. In a spiritual context those sources are ontological, experiential, and faith-based insights. Next, the philosophies of the perspectives of inquiry were provided in order that an educational leader can understand more fully where some of these spiritual ideas are based. Ethical norms of the classical worldview and modern worldview were discussed. This led to a reflection paradigm that leaders can use. The question of God and spirituality is an important section of the first chapter, describing issues pertaining to the issue of God and the beliefs of individual educators and how this may affect leadership. Next, the scientific elements of spirituality were briefly discussed as they may pertain to schools. Leaders must have background information about scientific research as it pertains to curriculum in school. (Note that a more complete explanation of scientific research can be found in Appendix A.) The issues of evil and moral education followed, which is appropriate for leaders as they continue to make decisions concerning "right and wrong." Finally, the chapter concludes with a discussion of the purposes of writing the book.

ILLUSTRATION: A CASE OF PERSONAL BELIEF

The Setting

Arlington is a suburb of Saint Louis, Missouri. It is contiguous to the city and was founded in the early 1890s. The people who settled there were dairy farmers of German descent. As the city of Saint Louis expanded in population, most of the farmers sold large sections of their property to developers who constructed houses similar to those in the city. They are made of brick produced by the clay mines that once flourished in the southwest section of Saint Louis. The houses are equally divided into single family dwellings and two family flats. However, there are some four family flats interspersed throughout the neighborhoods. There are some apartment buildings, but most are single- and two-family residences.

Businesses occupied buildings at street corners and all along major streets; all were small businesses which included grocery stores, pharmacies, bakeries, barber shops, restaurants, and taverns. Dentists, physicians, and attorneys had offices above the stores.

In the 1940s, the population suddenly began to change because of the migration of people from the city of Saint Louis. The city demolished a large section of substandard housing in a particular neighborhood called Mill Creek. Some of the houses even had outdoor plumbing, and all of the dwellings were built in the absence of housing codes. As the community became more prosperous, many moved to other areas in the city and to the suburbs. The people who moved into Mill Creek were economically depressed African Americans.

High-rise public housing buildings were erected to replace the houses which were destroyed. As many as fifty families were housed in a given apartment building. Of course, many people who had lived in the single-family houses and the two-family flats refused to live in the apartments and moved to nearby suburbs. Almost all of the families were receiving federal housing allowances. There was a chain reaction whereby most of the European Americans living in Arlington moved to the suburbs forming the second border immediately adjacent to Arlington and the other first borders of towns and villages.

The boundaries of the Arlington School District are coterminous with the boundaries of the town of Arlington. It is a school district with an enrollment of 5,315 students in 4 elementary schools (kindergarten through Grade 5); 2 middle schools (Grades 6–8); and a high school (Grades 9–12). The district employs 526 teachers. Arlington School District has a relatively stable enrollment with an operating budget that is adequate.

The board of education comprises 7 members elected at-large; 4 of the board members are European Americans and 3 members are African Americans. The pupil population is approximately 95% African American and the resident population is approximately 80% African American. The European Americans remaining in Arlington are either too poor to find other housing or are committed to living in an integrated setting. The European Americans on the board of education are from the latter group. There are many parents in the school who are supportive of educational opportunities for their children.

The drug problem is severe in the Arlington School District. In addition, gangs are very active in the community and in the schools.

Gang members supply most of the drugs used by students. Violence is a part of everyday life for most of the students not only at home and in the neighborhoods but also at school. Some of the houses and most of the buildings where businesses once flourished are vacant and have become places for gang members to hang out, sell drugs, and hide out. The substantial brick buildings, which had withstood the ravages of time and neglect, have become the domain of the gangs. Gang members have accepted the probability that they will die at a relatively young age either from drug abuse, AIDS, or from violence.

The Situation

The superintendent of schools, Dr. Richard Berkeley, is finishing his second year as superintendent in Arlington. Dr. Berkeley had been the assistant superintendent for curriculum in a suburban school district adjacent to the Atlanta, Georgia, school district. The board of education was certain that Dr. Berkeley was the right person to lead the district. In hiring Dr. Berkeley, the board had given him two mandates: update the entire curriculum, particularly in the areas of mathematics, science, and technology; and put on notice a group of teachers who were ineffective. The board had received numerous complaints from parents over the years about some teachers who had been with the district for many years but who were resistant to change and basically just putting in time until they could retire. Students graduating from Arlington scored very low on the SAT and ACT tests, which the board of education attributed to ineffective teaching and an outdated curriculum. Dr. Berkeley had been a high school physics teacher before he became an administrator and was especially dismayed at the outdated science curriculum.

Spirituality

There is a dimension to Dr. Berkeley which permeates most of his decision making. He had been raised in a very religious family. Both his parents regularly attended an evangelistic fundamentalist church which preached a literal interpretation of the Bible. When he was in college, Dr. Berkeley was exposed to an evolutionary approach to creation which caused him to question a significant number of his beliefs, including a literal interpretation of the book of Genesis. From that point on, he considered himself an agnostic. He had not dismissed belief in God entirely but found it difficult to believe the tenets of the faith he had been taught as a child.

When Dr. Berkeley was the assistant superintendent for curriculum in his previous position, the director of pupil personnel services reported to him. The director was a very articulate person who passionately sought after and explored all possible solutions to the ever increasing problem of student alcohol and drug abuse. Ultimately, she was unsuccessful. This affected Dr. Berkeley's thinking particularly about the people who sold drugs to students. It was especially difficult for him to understand how drug pushers could sell drugs to elementary age children.

Dr. Berkeley's agnosticism developed into atheism because he could not believe in the existence of an all-powerful and all-loving God who would permit such things to take place. Dr. Berkeley was married and had two children; in spite of his personal lack of belief, he and his family belonged to a church similar to the one in which he had grown up. He wanted his children to develop into people of good will and people who would lead a life of virtue. He believed that belonging to a church and attending services was a way to reinforce the values he and his wife were teaching their children at home. These values had served him well in his private life and in his career. Living a virtuous life was the key to success in this existence. Because he did not believe in God or in an afterlife, living a virtuous life was its own reward. Further, because this is the only life that a person will experience, he or she must utilize to the fullest extent possible whatever advantages become available.

The Problem

Rather than delegating the responsibility of reviewing and updating the science curriculum, Dr. Berkeley personally reviewed the instructional guides and textbooks used in the high school science program. Even though the goals and objectives were written in the appropriate format, the content of the science curriculum needed significant updating. The amazing discoveries that took place over the last ten years were nowhere to be found in the curriculum.

Dr. Berkeley thought that the exclusion of recent discoveries in both the curriculum and textbooks warranted his immediate attention. Further, some of the science teachers were those individuals identified by the board of education as being ineffective. It was April when he decided that the sad state of the science program was sufficient reason to terminate the employment of three tenured high school science teachers. He did not ask for support in rewriting the curriculum; nor did he inquire as to why the teachers were so ineffective.

The board of education supported Dr. Berkeley's recommendation to dismiss the teachers, but within a month all three teachers sued the school district alleging that their procedural due process rights had been violated. During the summer months, Dr. Berkeley finished revising the physics curriculum and purchased new textbooks. The science teachers throughout the Arlington School District all signed a petition calling for the resignation of Dr. Berkeley because he had not followed his own administrative procedures for updating the curriculum and purchasing new textbooks. The guidelines called for the involvement of building administrators, teachers, parents, and students when the curriculum was deemed to be in need of review by the superintendent. A committee was to be appointed by the superintendent who would review the curriculum and supporting instructional materials after which the committee would make recommendations to the superintendent who, in turn, would make a recommendation to the board of education.

Over the summer months, the science teachers gained the support of a small but vocal group of parents, and during the first semester of the new academic year this group attended every board meeting and spoke before the board, accusing Dr. Berkeley of forcing his personal beliefs on the science teachers and the children of the school district. The curriculum which Dr. Berkeley developed and the textbooks which he selected supported the big bang theory of how the universe was formed and further set forth that fossils evidence proved that human-like creatures existed for approximately two million years.

Discernment Questions

1. Did Dr. Berkeley's beliefs influence the manner in which he handled the dismissal of the science teachers?

2. Did Dr. Berkeley's beliefs influence the manner in which he revised the science curriculum?

3. What in Dr. Berkeley's beliefs justified disregarding his own procedures for curriculum review?

4. What are some of the ethical or cultural norms of the school?

5. Did spirituality influence Dr. Berkeley positive or negatively in this particular case?

6. Explain the reflection paradigm that Dr. Berkeley could have used in this situation.

7. How does the issue of evil contribute to the actions of the people in the case study?

8. Are Dr. Berkeley's personal conflicting issues with spirituality a problem in his leadership?

Conversations About the Case Study

The two major tasks given to Dr. Berkeley were to update the curriculum and eliminate ineffective teachers. Dr. Berkeley confused these two items when he mixed them together. The outdated curriculum did not necessarily mean that the high school science teachers were ineffective. The teachers could have been ineffective, but the means to assess their ineffectiveness were never exercised. Dr. Berkeley should have approached the ineffectiveness of the teachers as a separate matter and used other means of assessment such as observation of the teachers in question and discussions with the high school principal and science department. Even if

Dr. Berkeley had a suspicion that the three ineffective teachers were part of the reason the curriculum was out of date, he should have proved his assertions by using evidence-based assessments of their teaching and curriculum development ideas.

Regarding the curriculum, Dr. Berkeley was not using good management skills by taking on the task himself. An effective superintendent is one who can delegate and empower effective teachers and leaders to rework curriculum. It would appear that quite possibly he had a vested interest in which curriculum was chosen—quite possibly from his own agnostic beliefs that had developed over time. Because Dr. Berkeley was both a science teacher and religious person at one time, he should have been well aware of the many theories of the creation and/or development of the world, and the arguments that have followed in other schools about the science versus religion debate. He should have researched what other schools in the area or state had done in the past regarding science curriculum. But he also should have asked for teacher leaders and committee formation to help in assessing fairly what curricula are available and which aspects should be included. Therefore, Dr. Berkeley needed to use good management skills for both the assessment of the curriculum and the assessment of the teachers despite personal religious beliefs.

EXERCISE:
TOO RELIGIOUS OR NOT?

From the following examples, decide which could be "too religious" for a public school, and which would be appropriate considering the strong separation of church and state in our public schools. In other words, which situations could warrant an ethical, factual, or spiritual discussion without promoting a religious ideal? For further discussion, provide scenarios where a "not too religious" example could cross the line into being "too religious." How would you, as an administrator, handle each situation as it was discussed by students, teachers, or parents in your school?

1. A unit in an elementary classroom in December where a variety of religious celebrations are discussed including Kwanza, Christmas, and Hanukkah.

_____

_____

_____

2. A lecture about the basis for the Church of Scientology in a high school social studies class.

_____

_____

_____

3. An assignment in a high school English class requiring students to write about a hero in their life. An example provided included a previously written paper about Jesus as that person's hero.

_____

_____

_____

4. Learning "Away in a Manger" in an elementary music class.

_____

_____

_____

5. Discussing the three following topics in a science classroom: evolution, creationism, and intelligent design.

_____

_____

_____

6. A junior high school counselor encourages students to attend the Church of Christ to help in their spiritual formation.

_____

_____

_____

7. A high school history teacher takes on an additional job as Assistant Pastor in his church.

_____

_____

_____

8. Allowing an after-school Bible study group on school property and advised by a school teacher.

_____

_____

_____

9. Discussion of the Koran and the Bible in a high school history course.

_____

_____

_____

10. Having a "chocolate bunny exchange" in an elementary classroom at Easter.

_____

_____

_____

CHAPTER TWO
=====

The Personal Context of Experience, Reflection, and Beliefs

CHAPTER OBJECTIVES

- To identify how human spirituality develops within the context of educational leadership
- To explain how the psychological dimension of humans can influence the spirituality of educational leaders
- To describe how the various schools of psychology are complementary to each other and to the spirituality of educational leaders
- To explore how the personal spiritual life of educational leaders will affect their professional lives
- To explain how educational leaders can take control of their spirituality through exercising their freedom, practicing virtues, and living balanced lives
- To explore how educational leaders can enhance their spirituality in the face of adversity, conflict, and suffering.

THE CONTEXT

This chapter is divided into two sections. All human activities, both mental and physical, have a psychological dimension. The context of this chapter is centered on well-established personality theories and attempts to explain how spirituality is dependent on an understanding of the human psyche. Further, advancing in the spiritual life requires a person to face certain issues in personality development. Thus the first section is devoted to an explanation of the three schools of thought that inform our current and common understanding of human psychology.

The second section deals with the relationship that exists between a person's private life and his or her public leadership life. In fact, the private lives of people are the foundation of their professional lives in the sense that personal values and beliefs have a definite effect on the manner in which principals, superintendents, and other administrators practice the leadership profession. Spirituality cannot be left at home when a person leaves for his or her office. The second section explores key issues that most people will face that could shape their perspective on leadership.

PSYCHOLOGICAL FOUNDATIONS

There are three major approaches to the psychology of human spirituality. The first is the psychodynamic approach that attempts to explain personality and how it influences the decisions of educational leaders. The second approach to the psychology of human spirituality is the humanistic approach. The way in which people understand themselves has a significant effect on the way they develop human relationships. All human relationships have either a beneficial or detrimental effect on people. The third approach is the cognitive-behavioral approach. Behavior is influenced by a range of good and negative experiences; the reaction of educational leaders to those experiences influences how they will react in future situations.[1]

Psychodynamic Foundations of Educational Leadership Spirituality

The principles of psychoanalytic theory were first proclaimed by Sigmund Freud. Those principles have had a tremendous impact on the spirituality of professional human relationships. In fact, most other theories are either modifications to or reactions against what Freud set forth as the dynamics of human personality. For educational administrators, psychodynamic principles help to explain human motivation, which is a prerequisite to understanding the spiritual dimension of leadership.[2] There are many distinct theories in the psychodynamic approach, but those of Sigmund Freud, Carl Jung, and Alfred Adler seem to be the most relevant for educational leadership.

The following psychodynamic issues can influence the practice of educational leadership spirituality:

- The attitudes and perceptions of most people have been influenced by their early childhood experiences.
- There is a subconscious dimension to the human personality that is a reservoir of memories, emotions, desires, and impulses, which influence the attitudes and perceptions of most people.
- The generalized phenomenon of anxiety that is so prevalent in people today is probably caused by the content of their subconscious when it breaks into their consciousness.
- Everyone has psychological defense mechanisms that help to alleviate threatening thoughts and feelings.
- People tend to transfer their subconscious memories, emotions, desires, and impulses onto other people.
- Most people have a predisposition for certain strong emotional perceptions that are universal, such as the objectification of a person's idea of his or her self, which are commonly referred to as the collective unconscious.
- Every action that a person takes has purpose because humans are self-determining, creative, and dynamic.[3]

Humanistic Foundations of Educational Leadership Spirituality

All approaches to educational leadership spirituality are humanistic because they are focused on the relationships that exist between people as the milieu within which their spirituality is played out. As such, the humanistic approach emphasizes the ability of each person to determine his or her own destiny. Thus the strength of an individual's intellect and will are more important than a person's past history and environment in determining his or her decision making. From this perspective, a person's psychological well-being and his or her ability to create a personal spiritual perspective on educational leadership is dependent on how he or she relates to his or her own sense of self.

The existential approach is the most philosophical of all psychological approaches and has roots in the philosophies of Søren Kierkegaard, Friedrich Nietzsche, Edmund Husserl, Martin Heidegger, Karl Jaspers, and Jean-Paul Sartre, as well as a number of well known theologians, novelists, and playwrights. Perhaps the best description of the existential approach is the notion that every person is responsible for his or her own existence as the choosing subject. Thus the individual becomes capable of reflecting on events and attributing meaning to them, which enhances each person's consciousness of his or her existence. Such consciousness naturally leads to an awareness of the potential that such an existence offers for effecting life's direction.[4]

Client-centered psychology was developed by Carl Ransom Rogers. The fundamental orientation of this approach to psychology is that people are rational, socialized, forward-moving, and realistic. Thus such human emotions as jealousy and aggression are symptomatic of frustrations encountered in satisfying basic human needs such as love and security. However, people are basically good and try to be cooperative and trustworthy. In this sense, people can become self-actualizing because they are capable of exercising self-regulation by balancing their negative impulses against positive ways of meeting their needs.[5]

The following humanistic issues can influence the practice of educational leadership spirituality:

- People are decision makers and are capable of changing their lives through the choices they make.
- When people make decisions, they are exercising not only their human freedom but also their values because all actions are value-laden.

- Ultimately, everyone is alone in his or her decision making and thus responsible for the choices made.
- Human spirituality is transcendental in the sense that it fosters beliefs and values, which are beyond a person's immediate needs and experiences.
- People are self-actualizing through which they exercise their rationality.
- People are self-regulating through which they can control their attitudes and emotions.
- The ultimate goal of humans is to become a fully functioning person.[6]

Cognitive-Behavioral Foundations of Educational Leadership Spirituality

Underlying the cognitive-behavioral approach is the assumption that knowing the causes of human behavior does not necessarily facilitate behavioral change. The objective of utilizing the cognitive-behavioral approach is empowerment. It gives people control over their actions and ultimately over their life. In order to take control, it is necessary for people to program their thoughts in such a way that they will be able to practice a change in their behavior. In the cognitive-behavioral school of thought, there are four theories: behavioral, rational emotive, cognitive, and reality.

The forerunner of all behavioral theories is Ivan Pavlov. However, the major creators of what is practiced today are B. F. Skinner, Albert Bandura, and Joseph Wolpe. Behavioral theories rest on the experience of *reinforcement*: the consequences of behavior increase the possibility that a given behavior will be performed again or, without the consequences, the behavior could be extinguished. In this context, reinforcement is also the basis of motivation theory. Thus when a reward follows a behavior and the behavior is increased, there is positive reinforcement. Likewise, not attending to certain behaviors is a way of extinguishing unwanted behaviors. Eventually, a person's behavior becomes generalized as a consequence of certain reinforcement that he or she received in a prior situation.[7]

Albert Ellis developed the rational emotive approach, which sets forth the notion that most problems in life arise not from situations but from the way in which people view situations. A central aspect of his approach is the importance of pleasure, which he viewed as a major goal in life. The focus, of course, is on long-term rather than short-term pleasures. Even though biological, social, and other factors contribute to long-term life pleasures, the rational emotive approach is predicated on rationalism, the correct way of thinking.[8]

Aaron Beck's cognitive psychology is also concerned with the impact that thinking has on a person's behavior. He placed particular emphasis on automatic thoughts, which are those thoughts that people may not be fully conscious of, but which are an outgrowth of a person's cognitive schemata. This is important because a person's schemata is what he or she uses in making choices and in drawing inferences about his or her life. Of course, automatic thoughts produce emotional reactions, physiologic reactions, and behaviors.[9]

William Glasser developed reality therapy, which is primarily concerned with the way people perceive reality because such perception determines their feelings, thoughts, and actions. Thus it is not reality, but rather the perception of reality that is important. In turn, people try to control the world and their part of that world through behavior that will satisfy their basis needs of belonging, power, freedom, and enjoyment. Of course, people can try to control their worldview in an appropriate or inappropriate manner. For example, they may choose to be angry or depressed rather than accepting and forgiving.[10]

The following cognitive-behavioral issues can influence the practice of educational leadership spirituality:

- When humans experience a positive consequence that follows a behavior, they are likely to continue the behavior.
- When humans experience a negative consequence that follows a behavior, they are likely to discontinue the behavior.
- Positive behavior is increased by performance accomplishment, vicarious experiences, verbal persuasion, and lowering emotional reactions.
- Most human problems emanate from the way that people view other people, things, and events.
- Rationalistic thinking can change a person's behavior.

- Everyone experiences automatic/spontaneous thoughts that can produce emotional reactions and changes in behaviors.
- People are capable of controlling their behaviors, which is how people can satisfy their needs.[11]

Practical Discussions and Examples

The best administrators and leaders embrace humanistic spirituality. In particular, a successful leader stands behind all decisions made and reinforces those decisions that may have been incorrect as a fault of his or her leadership. Humanistic spirituality emphasizes the ability of each person to determine his or her own destiny. Therefore, when a person becomes an administrator, he or she is choosing a role in which daily decision making affects hundreds of people. He or she further exercises this approach in knowing that he or she is alone in decision making and thus responsible for the choices made. This is true in relationships with others as well. The manner in which an administrator speaks and treats others in a community reflects upon leadership ability—actions for which he or she must be held responsible.

For example, suppose that at a teacher meeting, the principal asks for some input from the teachers about what can be done to improve student achievement. One teacher in particular voices loudly the disappointment she has in the lack of resources offered by the school and principal for her classroom. She states that a teacher could teach much more effectively with adequate supplies, a teaching aide, and newer textbooks. The principal gets upset by these remarks, and proceeds to shout at the teacher (psychodynamic spirituality) because he is angry. However, his actions were not appropriate since the room was filled with teachers. The teachers would learn (behavioral spirituality) not to speak up when asked a question because they would be worried about how they might be treated in front of others. Furthermore, the principal now faces difficult leadership techniques because he must live with the consequences of his actions (humanistic spirituality). It would be more advantageous for the principal to acknowledge his error and encourage feedback as needed. Likewise, the outspoken teacher may need to self-reflect on her approach to this situation because she too must live with the consequences of being so aggressive to the principal in front of other teachers. Using the cognitive-behavioral approach, both the teacher and principal should practice a change in their behavior in order to empower themselves to be effective teachers and leaders.

While an administrator may bring personal beliefs and spirituality to his or her decision making, he or she must assure himself or herself and others that the choices he or she is making is for the good of all involved. Furthermore, as administrators make continual decisions, they will learn what works for them in their situation and often follow a similar path. This is why some administrators have difficulty changing positions to a new environment that may be very different from that last one. Behaviors need to change accordingly, and an administrator who cannot do so successfully will have more difficulty. For example, an administrator who successfully led a parent group each week in his last school may have difficulty doing so in a new school where many of the parents may work in shifts at local factories. The administrator must not judge but learn to find new ways to reach these parents if his goal is to benefit the students.

THE ELEMENTS OF A PERSONAL SPIRITUALITY FOR EDUCATIONAL LEADERS

Most people are event-driven in the sense that they take stock of their personhood when confronted with a significant and meaningful event. Some of the most meaningful events are marriage, the birth of a son or daughter, a milestone birthday, the death of a friend or relative, a divorce, or being terminated from work. The purpose for reflecting on significant events is usually to invest personal meaning and purpose in life. This meaningfulness factor is very difficult to analyze, but it is a common human phenomenon.

The Search for Meaning[12]

Perhaps one of the most important written expressions of the search for meaning can be found in the works of the noted psychiatrist and author, Viktor Frankl—specifically in his book, *Man's*

Search for Meaning: An Introduction to Logotherapy. He epitomized the struggle for meaning in his own personal life journey because his parents, brother, and wife were victims of the Holocaust. He and his sister were the only two members of his entire family who survived the concentration camps.

In fact, it was Frankl's opinion that the search for meaning is the primary motivator in life. Further, the notion of meaning is unique to each person and because of that uniqueness, meaning can be found only by the individual himself or herself. The expression of meaning is found in ideals and values. Frankl used the phrase *the will to meaning* as the fundamental principle for finding meaning not only in significant life events but also in everyday life. Meaningfulness becomes the pathway to personal freedom and the sustaining element along that pathway.

Each person's profession or occupation is directly related to his or her search for meaning. This is particularly true in the service professions like teaching and educational leadership. Even though superintendents and principals engage in work in order to make a living, it is also obvious that many, if not most of them fulfill their professional responsibilities with a sense of purpose and meaning that enhances their private lives. It is certainly tragic to see some educational administrators who no longer possess meaningfulness in their professional lives. Sometimes without knowing and realizing it, they can either detract from or enhance the lives of faculty members, staff members, students, and parents depending on the degree of purposefulness that they exhibit in carrying out their responsibilities.

Frankl was also concerned with the existential moment, because he thought that the search for meaning must be grounded in the reality of the here and now. Thus the external environment rather than the person's psyche is the milieu within which each person can find the meaning of life.

Finally, Frankl had a deep understanding of how personal relationships can shape an individual's search for meaning. He certainly professed the importance of love, both in the platonic and intimate senses, and how it connects one person to another. In fact, it is correct to assert that human relations are the conduit through which people find meaning in life. In a very interesting way, Frankl understood that human potentiality to form meaningful relationships can easily elude a person. He lamented the idea that the opportunity to actualize a person's potential is the only transitory aspect of life.

Frankl coined a phrase that summarizes his philosophy and psychology of life: *tragic optimism*. Even though human existence and life is constantly filled with suffering, he believed that people are capable of growing beyond their sufferings and can change not only themselves but also their environment and even the world.

Human Suffering[13]

One of the most persistent and universal experiences of humanity is suffering. No human being can escape this existential reality, which is a shared phenomenon that can become a vehicle for human sympathy and understanding. However, it is also a private phenomenon, because no one can truly alleviate the suffering of another person. Suffering is different than pain. Suffering arises from personal or symbiotic experience and, as opposed to pain, cannot be alleviated through medication and other therapies.

It is difficult to define suffering; rather, it is easier to describe the circumstance that is produced because of suffering. Typically, suffering begs the questions: Why me? Thus, there is usually a sense of victimization, anguish, and meaninglessness in the human response to suffering. Symbiotic suffering is generally a response of people to the suffering of others; it is a certain felt kinship.

For example, the principal, teachers, and staff members from a school will typically experience symbiotic suffering when a child attending their school is injured or dies because of an accident or act of violence. Those teachers and staff members who had close professional contact with the child will suffer more than those who only had a passing relationship to the child.

All people of goodwill suffer from the horrendous tragedy of the Holocaust, from racism, from spouse and child abuse, and from large scale natural disasters such as floods and tornados. Of course nonvictims suffer to a lesser extent than those who personally experienced the tragedy. Thus people live on a continuum, existing somewhere between meaningfulness and happiness on one end and meaninglessness and sorrow on the other end.

Superintendents, principals, and other administrators can make a positive or negative response to their own sufferings and to the sufferings of others, which is of particular concern because of the effect that perceived suffering has on children and young adults in their character formations. The manner in which adults encounter suffering can have a moral force in the school community that could model responses that children and others should make in regard to suffering.

Self-agency is a response that people can make to suffering that emphasizes a person's beliefs, intentions, and actions. An individual's own personal life history allows him or her to become self-determining. Because suffering changes a person, it can have an enhancing or destructive effect, depending on how the individual perceives the suffering event.

Using life narrative is a technique that utilizes a person's ongoing historical account of successes, failures, happiness, and suffering. In this way, suffering is viewed as a condition of life that becomes a part of a person's life narrative. In developing a life narrative, the following guidelines could help a person determine the effectiveness of his or her response to suffering. First, the narrative must be empowering in order to release people from destructive alternatives. Second, the narrative must help people to see through current distortions. Third, the narrative must have the power to keep people from resorting to violence. Finally, the narrative must help people to transform the suffering into meaning.

Some people falsely believe that life is bearable only when they are free from suffering. However, in the face of tragedy, people often rise to greater heights than they thought possible of themselves. For example, the news media is constantly reporting the voluntary responses of principals, teachers, and staff members to human needs such as raising money for students and their parents who have extraordinary medical bills or no health insurance.

The response of people to such situations is predicated on human freedom. People have choices and are not obliged to help others. A solemn and relevant treatise on freedom and responsibility was written by Jean-Paul Sartre. He believed that people initiate everything in the world, and thus they are also responsible for the good and evil that is everywhere in human experience. Of course, what he was trying to avoid is blaming extraneous forces for the human condition.

Rather, he asserted people must recognize that they share in the responsibility and, in fact, are ultimately alone in the decisions they make. Further, the decisions that an individual makes will have an impact on whom he or she becomes as a person since all decisions are value-laden.

Practical Discussions and Examples

Every administrator will have to deal with tragedy in his or her career. Most likely, every administrator will have to deal with it on a personal level as well as in response to a school or community tragedy. Death, tragedy, life, and happiness are all part of a person's experience. How an administrator handles all of these situations reflects the nature of the school and community. If an administrator is empathetic and helpful to others, then in turn, his or her staff and students begin to follow suit. In general, most schools operate at a positive or happy level; although rarely would every individual in a school be happy since various individuals may be suffering at any given point. An administrator should be aware of individual issues of tragedy in addition to aiding in any major tragedy that affects multiple people in a school. Thus if a crisis happens, an administrator can help lead others through it and hopefully end up back at a equilibrium or a state similar to before the tragedy (rarely would people return to an equal state if they were affected by tragedy, but eventually they can return to a state where they can work and function moderately happy).

An administrator should be aware of and provide aid for, if possible, an individual tragedy, such as a student whose parent has just been diagnosed with terminal cancer. A personal conversation with the parent, teacher, and child would be beneficial, as would a personal note from the administrator to the family or child. Also, if a teacher in a building is ill and has health complications, an administrator should be supportive of the teacher and encourage him or her to take as much time as needed. Too often, students, parents, and teachers feel that schools and administrators are there only to enforce rules. An administrator who shows compassion, empathy, and support in times of trauma for others will, in the end, have a stronger school and community while retaining good teachers, parents, and students.

For example, one teacher who had complications with pregnancy felt bad because she would have to leave school suddenly to go to the hospital or to see her doctor for an unscheduled visit. An empathetic and thoughtful administrator drove her to the hospital, and an equally thoughtful resource teacher took over her class at the last minute. These types of actions lead to a positive learning and working environment. Furthermore, it takes little effort from the administrator to show this compassion.

An administrator can also lead effectively by making sure that there are enough counselors and support personnel to aid the school and staff in the event of a tragedy. When a major catastrophe occurs, approximately ten times the number of people directly affected claim to have problems or psychological distress. Basic things an administrator can do to aid in situations like this is to be as prepared ahead of time as possible with a crisis plan and intervention strategies for those students needing help. In a school year, administrators will have to implement supplemental support for issues like a student dying, a student or teacher committing suicide, a major car accident of a student or parent, and so forth. A strong but empathetic leader is needed so that the school community can recover as best possible.

Taking Control of Your Spiritual Life

The search for meaning is a journey that requires educational leaders to equip themselves with resources in order to be successful. For centuries, the moral virtues of *prudence, justice, fortitude,* and *temperance* have provided seekers with assistance in taking control of their spiritual lives, which is the prerequisite for finding meaning in life. In contrast to past definitions of the virtues, the contemporary view underscores the importance of human development, which is the process that begins in early childhood, extends into adulthood, and finally terminates only with death.

Erik Erikson's concept of human growth emphasizes a critical transition from one stage to the next. It is important for each person to resolve certain crises that usually occur during each of the stages, which prepare individuals for the next stage. In fact, without a positive resolution of the typical crisis that occurs in a given stage, further development becomes problematic.

The stages do not have discrete periods of demarcation, but rather should be considered as a continuum. Each person experiences the stages in varying degrees of intensity, and different people may even oscillate between the stages. Erikson's eight stages of moral development with their corresponding crises are as follows:

Stages	Crises
Stage One: Infancy	Basic Trust vs. Basic Mistrust
Stage Two: Early Childhood	Autonomy vs. Shame, Doubt
State Three: Play Age	Initiative vs. Guilt
Stage Four: School Age	Industry vs. Inferiority
Stage Five: Adolescence	Identity vs. Identity Confusion
Stage Six: Young Adult	Intimacy vs. Isolation
Stage Seven: Adulthood	Generativity vs. Stagnation
Stage Eight: Old Age	Integrity vs. Despair [14]

Lawrence Kohlberg was another researcher who tried to demonstrate the importance of human moral development, which he set forth into six stages. Further he held the position that the six stages are universal to all people. He also believed that basic human moral development is not related to specific religious beliefs; rather, humans develop morally through their positive or negative engagements with the environment and with other people.[15]

From this developmental perspective of human growth, educational leaders can grasp a better understanding of the moral virtues. It is difficult to define the term *virtue*, and it is more appropriate to describe virtues in a functional manner. Thus virtues are qualities that shape people into integrated persons; by their very nature, virtues are flexible and adaptable to the milieu in which people must act. Through practice, the virtues shape human inclinations and dispositions to act in a certain way. Because the virtues are acquired in a similar manner to the way athletes and musicians acquire their abilities and develop their talents, they must be cultivated over time in order to facilitate a certain way of acting. Thus the virtues help educational leaders arrive at good moral judgments with ease.[16]

Prudence

The foundational virtue is prudence because it is exercised in concrete situations and permeates all decision making. Prudence includes the following aspects: memory, foresight, imagination, and docility. Thus the prudent person tries to recall past and similar experiences when he or she was faced with an issue or problem that required a decision. The prudent person then attempts to predict possible consequences associated with the pending decision. He or she develops alternatives to solving the problem or handling the issue. The prudent person is open to learning from others and from former situations, which is a key aspect of this virtue.

Justice

Justice is concerned with an individual's relationship to others in the communities in which he or she lives. There are three kinds of justice. Distributive justice is concerned with the obligations that societies have toward individuals. The justice that is required of individuals to the societies in which they live is commonly referred to as legal justice. Commutative justice regulates the relationships which exist among individuals. All relationships create rights and responsibilities upon each individual and the societies to which these belong. The overriding issue with justice is that there is a corresponding responsibility for each right.

Fortitude

Everyone in our contemporary society is confronted with pressures that emerge in the form of anxiety and fearfulness. The virtue of fortitude helps people moderate their fear and anxiety, and also helps individuals overcome their weaknesses in the pursuit of doing good in their private and public lives. A weakness that is manifested through fear of making commitments can paralyze a person, and fears of criticism, failure, disappointment, and humiliation can also devastate an individual. Thus, fortitude helps people overcome obstacles and strengthens them to act beyond their fears in pursuing what they believe to be the right course of action.

Temperance

There are people who are obsessed with their professional responsibilities. Some may even place their work ahead of the welfare not only of themselves but also of their families. Human desire for pleasures and comforts are truly good in themselves because, without such desires, people eventually blunt their sensibilities for anything except the knowledge that they have completed their professional responsibilities. People on the other extreme indulge so much in pleasures that they neglect their responsibilities or perform them at a minimal level. Thus temperance is a flexible virtue that requires individuals to learn their limits in order to recognize when gratification begins to obscure other values.[17]

Because the notions of good and evil play such a central role in spiritual development, Appendix B has been written for the person who wants a more in depth understanding of this universal phenomenon.

Practical Discussions and Examples

An administrator is seen as the ultimate leader in a school—someone who should be held in high regard with high moral standards and expectations of all. Therefore, an administrator should be at the highest stages of moral development and continually push his or her students and faculty to also learn and reach a high level of moral development. A common complaint in America's schools has been the lack of character education or moral upbringing. Many complain that this has been a problem because of the lack of religion in the public schools; however, as an educational leader, one should be able to express and teach high moral regard without necessarily espousing religion—thus spirituality affects the administrator.

An administrator must be "at home" with himself or herself and have a strong sense of right versus wrong. Many leaders lead by example. Therefore, if an educational leader must make difficult decisions, he or she must be comfortable with the choices made based on his or her own moral values. For example, in one high school the discipline policy indicates that any person in the high school who is caught drinking alcohol is automatically dismissed from any extracurricular teams or clubs for the remainder of the semester. Suppose that in August the entire football team has a party, and when the police arrive, ten of the main players are arrested for underage consumption of alcohol. Should the administrator follow the rules and dismiss all those charged players from the team? What if the community is outraged and feels that it was a "set up" in order to eliminate a football team that had a promising season? What if the administrator does not personally agree with the law stating that the legal drinking age is 21 and older? An administrator must be able to follow through with a decision that is based in moral values that would ultimately affect others in a positive way. Therefore, while the administrator may not agree with the law, he or she must follow the law and uphold the school regulations concerning this law.

A different issue related to personal spirituality is the spirituality affecting a leader's personal life away from school. Most would agree that administrators work long hours and often feel like their home is the school. They may even have to deal with issues at their family home, taking phone calls in the middle of the night or attending unexpected meetings or events outside of normal school hours. An administrator must be careful to create a work-life balance where she or he is happy holding a professional role without neglecting family and vice versa. An administrator should feel free to lead a spiritual life in any way he or she chooses without consequences from the school or community; however, to achieve this, the administrator must be careful not to take personal spirituality "too far." For example, suppose that a vice principal is a deeply religious man who is a lay deacon and leader at his local Christian church. He hangs a large wooden cross around his rear view mirror in his car. Most know he is very religious because they have seen this car in the parking lot and have heard about his work in his church. This man's spirituality is probably heavily influenced by his religion, which in turn most likely affects his leadership. As long as he doesn't continue to talk about his religion in school or preach to others in the school, he should be free and proud of what he has chosen to personally satisfy his spiritual needs. Therefore, while spirituality is part of each person and can affect the way he or she carries on day to day, it is in the ways that person shows appreciation and compassion for self, families, and others with high morals that is important.

SUMMARY

First, the authors described the psychodynamic foundations of educational leadership spirituality followed by the humanistic foundations, including the existential approach. This discussion was followed by the cognitive-behavioral approach, with the assumption that knowing the causes of human behavior does not necessarily facilitate behavioral change. These are important concepts for educational leaders to understand when making decisions and implementing change. Next, searching for real meaning and understanding human suffering is discussed. An empathetic and compassionate educational leader can build a stronger learning community by helping students and staff through these issues. Next, information is provided on how to take control of a spiritual life and how it may carry into leadership. A balanced life is crucial to help maintain a positive equilibrium personally and professionally. Finally, the appendices discuss issues that administrators must understand in dealing with people from a variety of spiritual backgrounds: the issues of harm, tragedy, salvation, emancipation, and life after death.

ILLUSTRATION: A CASE OF PERSONAL SPIRITUALITY

The Setting

Weston Elementary School is a small, urban school in the city of Chicago. It was a large school at one time, in particular when the area was inhabited by wealthy individuals. Because it was so close to downtown, the area used to be inhabited in the 1950s and 1960s by families where typically the father commuted downtown to work each day on the "El" or "L"—the mass transit system in downtown Chicago where much of the track is elevated with little built underground. The community is lined with beautiful old apartment townhouses along tree-lined streets.

However, over time, many of the more affluent people moved to the suburbs as immigrants moved into the area. As some of those immigrants became wealthier, they also moved away leaving only poorer individuals. As this shift happened, housing prices began to plummet, and many poor Hispanic families began moving into the area because they could afford the property. While the architecture is still very nice, the streets are starting to look very run down and lined with trash. In particular, the area has recently become inundated with gang activity. The families who live there are working very hard with local police and community leaders to keep their streets safe and to keep gang violence down. Unfortunately, the efforts are not paying off, and gang violence is increasing in this area.

Weston Elementary is a beautiful old brick school, but because of the low enrollment compared to when it was built, the top floor of the school is closed and not safe for use. The school's enrollment is around 300 children. The school's documented racial distribution consists of Caucasian, African American, and Asian American students, but the majority are Hispanic—matching the community ethnic makeup. The rate of students eligible for free and reduced price lunch is 92%. The families in the school are generally very supportive since they are working hard to keep gang violence out of the community. They realize that focusing on the schools can be a way to reduce gang violence in the community. In particular, Weston Elementary is the only local elementary school in the area, and the parents and school leaders feel that they may lessen gang activity if they can teach young children not to get involved.

The problem, of course, is that gang violence is prevalent, and older students from the junior high and high school have threatened some of the elementary students. They have also tried to recruit some of the fourth and fifth grade students into the gangs. Furthermore, some of the students in the elementary school have older siblings who are currently involved in gang activities.

The Situation

Mr. Lopez is the principal of Weston Elementary, and he has watched this transition over the last five years as the area has become infiltrated with gang issues. He has worked with parents and community leaders regularly on a task force to keep gangs, gang violence, and gang issues out of his school. He has approved the use of metal detectors in his building, which means that all children, parents, visitors, and teachers must enter through the metal detectors each day. He has also worked hard at getting a uniform policy established in the hopes that students wearing uniforms might be left alone by gang members. The uniforms were donated by an organization in the city of Chicago. He has hired multiple security personnel, including night guards, to keep the building, grounds, and parking lots safe. He continues to meet with members of the community, including spiritual leaders, to see what measures he can take as an administrator to make his school as safe and gang-free as possible. The last meeting was the finalization of a school lock-down plan in the event of intruders with weapons into his school. Furthermore, the staff has just been trained in safety measures by holding a lock-down drill this week. Mr. Lopez and his community have worked together to do what they can for the safety of the children while trying to continue to teach the students to stay out of gangs.

Spirituality

Mr. Lopez considers himself a spiritual man. He and many of his community members have been raised in the Catholic faith. He regularly sees many of the parents and community leaders at Mass, and he is very comfortable with the positive teachings of the Church. While he considers himself religious, he does not impose his views or thoughts on his teachers or the school children because he realizes that while most may be Catholic, a number are not. Therefore, he works hard at being privately spiritual while publicly secular, making judgments based solely on what is best for his teachers and students. He realizes that there are many problems in the world and with children involved in gangs, and he is just trying his best to help those students he can.

The Problem

One day shortly after the safety drill, while with the teachers, Mr. Lopez notices a group of fifth graders entering the school building all dressed with black shirts wearing yellow and black caps. He realizes immediately that this dress is characteristic of the 15th Street Gang. He immediately brings the boys to his office and requires them to remove caps and change their shirts into the school uniform. He states that anything related to gangs is not allowed in his school, and that they should not be affiliated. Mr. Lopez then asks teachers to be vigilant today while he makes phone calls to the boys' parents. At the end of the school day, Mr. Lopez holds an emergency teacher meeting to receive feedback about the day. The teachers report that while they noticed some tension between these boys and some other boys in the school, there didn't seem to be anything problematic.

Mr. Lopez is relieved that this issue has been so well controlled by himself and his teachers. He leaves school that day hoping and praying that his school and community are moving one step closer to reducing the gang problems. He is awakened in the middle of the night by a police officer who calls to inform him that one of his fifth-grade students and one of his first-grade students (who were brothers) have been killed in a gang-related incident. They suspect the 15th Street Gang is responsible. When he arrives at school early the next morning to prepare his teachers, there is a large message on the building that had been spray painted. It says, "15th Street Gang Will Rule This School." Mr. Lopez completely breaks down. He is extremely angry, upset, scared, and exhausted. He and the police decide it is in the best interest of all to cancel school for the week.

Mr. Lopez decides to go to his priest immediately to talk of the situation. He and the priest speak for approximately three hours during which time Mr. Lopez describes his anger at God for allowing these things to happen; he describes his own lack of faith in religion since these things keep happening despite his good and correct efforts; he describes his desire to "throw in the towel" at this point in his career; and he can't understand how to appreciate his own religious beliefs when this is happening directly to his students. He no longer feels like he can be a pillar of strength because he is losing faith.

Discernment Questions

1. In what ways has personal spirituality changed for Mr. Lopez?

2. What kinds of spiritual conversations will Mr. Lopez need to have with his teachers and staff once school resumes?

3. How can Mr. Lopez, his teachers, and his community search for meaning in this situation?

4. Do you think Mr. Lopez will recover from this? In what ways can this type of situation make him weaker and stronger?

5. What strategies will Mr. Lopez need to use when school resumes?

6. What types of human suffering will community members and students experience?

Conversations About the Case Study

Mr. Lopez must first determine if he can recover from this situation and continue to lead the school effectively. He is personally beaten down, and while this is understandable, his school and the community will be looking for his leadership at this time. Mr. Lopez would benefit from talking with community spiritual leaders because he will be one of many who are extremely upset. It may help him understand how various members of this school will grieve and seek guidance from others. Will he recover? It is important for Mr. Lopez and others to realize that no one ever really recovers from a situation like this. Instead, he must address his feelings and encourage others to do the same.

Then, he should start making plans about how to turn this bad situation into positive outcomes. Having conversations with teachers and students about the negative issues related to gang violence should be a teaching lesson from this horrible tragedy. Mr. Lopez should also work closely with police to continue to try and reduce the impact of the gangs in the school. One way to begin the healing process may be to have a memorial service at school the first day it resumes. It would also be helpful to have school counselors and psychologists speak with teachers first and help those who are very upset, in addition to offering suggestions for teachers to aid students upon their return. These same counselors and psychologists should also be available the first few weeks of children returning to school.

In addition, Mr. Lopez should look at what is happening in his building. For example, he probably should have had more intervention than just requiring the students to change shirts if he suspected that gangs were having more of an impact in the school. He could have held a meeting with the children, their parents, community members, police, and a few teachers. He also could have police officers and school counselors lead a school assembly about the importance of safety in the children's lives at school and at home. Last, he needs to work with the police force in the area so that they can help each other stop violence before it begins.

EXERCISE:
SELF-ASSESSMENT OF PSYCHOLOGICAL DIMENSIONS

The following is a brief assessment of your orientation toward your own psychological dimensions. Personal dimensions are affected by upbringing, conversations with others, professional experience, and self reflection. This understanding should be helpful to you as you lead others in an educational setting. Please rate the degree to which you agree on a scale of 1 to 3 (1 = disagree, 2 = partially agree, 3 = agree). [18]

Humanistic Orientation

_____ I am personally responsible for all the decisions I make.

_____ I consider myself to be capable of self-actualization.

_____ I believe that most people are capable of working together.

_____ I believe that each person can determine his or her own destiny.

_____ I believe people are capable of self-reflection.

_____ I generally trust others.

_____ I believe people can overcome negative aspects of their past to function at a high level.

_____ I believe that most people want to be in control and charge of their own life.

_____ I believe people are able to cooperate—controlling their emotions.

_____ I believe people can change their lives based on decisions they make.

_____ **Rating** (A median score is 20)

Cognitive-Behavioral Orientation

_____ I believe empowerment gives people control over their actions.

_____ I believe reinforcement changes behavior.

_____ Positive behavior reinforces my rational thoughts.

_____ I believe in a correct way of approaching issues.

_____ In order for me to maintain balance, it is important to be logical and efficient in thought.

_____ I tend not to repeat an action if is has a negative consequence.

_____ The reactions I get from others influence my behaviors.

_____ Most conflicts occur because of the way people view others.

_____ I can change my perception of people and things with rational thought.

_____ Spontaneous thought can lead to emotional responses and reactions.

_____ **Rating** (A median score is 20)

CHAPTER THREE

The Nature of Educational Leadership Regarding Experience, Reflection, and Beliefs

CHAPTER OBJECTIVES

- To identify how human spirituality develops within the context of educational leadership
- To understand the role of spirituality in the educational leadership vocation
- To understand the role of spirituality in the learning community
- To explain how spirituality affects the research responsibility of the educational leader
- To explain how educational leaders can synthesize and analyze knowledge through their spirituality

THE EDUCATIONAL LEADERSHIP VOCATION

A vocation is a call to service as set forth in Chapter 2 in relation to personal commitments. In the context of this chapter, that call to service is further developed and is much more focused. For this presentation, a vocation is a call to provide services to members of a community. The call can be implicit or explicit and may impact members of many communities. For example, a physician has a call through his or her profession to heal members of the community where he or she practices medicine. If he or she accepts a position as a public health administrator, the community could be an entire city.

An accountant working for a company has a call from the employees, owner, and general public to provide ethical and competent services. What he or she does at work could impact not only the employees and owner but also the people who buy the products sold by the company.

An educational leader has an explicit call or vocation because he or she is contracted by the board of education to serve the citizens of a given school district through the administration of its educational programs. The members of the board of education are usually elected by the people of the community, and thus they intentionally exercise the call to service.

This use of the term *vocation* is different than the manner in which it has been historically used. It is common knowledge that the first use of the term was to designate a person as a religious who would minister to the members of a particular church. Further, at one time many communities thought that there are only three vocations: to the religious ministry, to the married state in life, and to the single life. All other endeavors were considered to be occupations or professions.

Today, the notion of vocation is synonymous with *purpose*. Thus the reason why a person either became or wants to become an educational administrator is the link to considering the educational leadership profession as a calling or vocation. That reason, however, must be selflessly motivated. Service should be the reason. Of course, it is impossible to bring the notion of service to such an extreme that the administrator ignores all other benefits of being a superintendent, principal, or other administrator. Certainly, the higher salary and the opportunity to make decisions that have a significant impact on the education of children are other reasons for wanting to be an educational leader. However, these cannot be the predominant reasons because there are considerable hardships that also come with great responsibility. Prestige, power, and money have never been strong enough motivators to endure the hardships that come with the position of educational leader.

Thus educational leaders are called to use their skills in order to best serve others and children in particular. Many teachers would state that they work in the field of education because of a desire to help children rather than for a monetary or selfish reason. Most give much more than what is expected, because they want to help as many children as possible. The same holds true for a school administrator. For example, school administrators know that they will need to work many long hours, deal with a variety of issues, and work in mediation and conflict resolution. By nature of the position, administrators are dealing with such diverse groups of people that they must find the best course of action benefiting the most people while trying to maintain harmony within the learning community.

Assumptions

There are a number of assumptions that underpin this perspective on educational leadership as a vocation. These assumptions are taken for granted by some people, but need to be explicated in order to clarify the notion of vocation.

- The first is the assumption that reality itself calls forth the educational leader to service. Even though most people would like some things in life to be different than they are, educational leaders must accept reality as it is with all its implications and without imposing on reality a distorted hopefulness. Thus the educational leader practices critical intentionality in making decisions about the reality of life. He or she refuses to act out of fear, personal biases, or imaginary hopefulness. Reality becomes the truth that grounds the goodness intended in decision making.
- The second assumption concerns the personal integrity development that emerges from making critical intentional decisions. As seekers of the truth in reality, educational leaders naturally self assess their motivation in trying to arrive at appropriate decisions. In essence they are searching for personal authenticity. The sources of this authenticity are

transcending values that are operational in the various communities to which the educational leader is a member. In our pluralistic society, the primary values of the local community, the state where the school district is located, and the values of the United States are the main sources from which decisions must emanate. Thus social justice, procedural due process, and representative collective negotiations are values that are present in those communities. In this context the authenticity of the educational leader is grounded in being a public person.[1]

- Third, vocation is a spiritual notion, because it is concerned with the purpose or purposes for which we live out our lives. Sometimes those purposes are in direct conflict with physical, economic, and social well-being, but are freely chosen for a higher good.

- The fourth assumption is the self-evident truth that people are not completely controlled by their physiology. Rather, we are also spiritual in nature and capable of transcending our corporeal instincts.

- The fifth assumption concerns the evidence which could indicate that a person may have chosen the wrong vocation. Feelings are indications of our inner health just as pain is an indication that something has afflicted our physical health. Chronic feelings of dissatisfaction with a person's responsibilities as an educational leader accompanied by feelings of meaninglessness, dissatisfaction, anger, disillusionment, or emptiness are certain indicators that a person should consider choosing another profession or position other than being an educational administrator.

The Reflection Mandate

The Content of Reflection

In this context there is a perennial question that has no definitive answer, but which should constantly inform and guide educational leaders as they reflect on their vocation: What does it mean to have the vocation of an educational leader?

While the answer to that question might seem obvious on first consideration, the potential answer is very complex. The content of possible reflection could begin in four areas. The first area is a realization that there are elements in the vocation of being an educational leader that are beyond a person's control. In a true sense the destiny of the educational leader is controlled by the needs of the community that he or she serves. Thus there is a considerable amount of ambiguity in what the future holds because the individual and collective needs of people are constantly in flux. No one definitively knows what the future will bring. The life of an educational leader is a work-in-progress.

The second area of reflection extends the ambiguity of the future into a realization that the developing life of students, faculty, and staff members, and the beliefs and values of the community free educational leaders from excessive self-interest. Superintendents, principals, and other administrators must be able to give into the needs of others as an integral part of their responsibilities. It is the other that takes precedence over self-interest.

The status of being an educational leader may not hold the same prestige as being a corporate executive, a politician, a physician, an attorney, or some other professions. Thus a third reflection might concern not only the benefits but also the deficits of being an educator.

For educational leaders that adhere to a belief in God or who belong to a faith community, the tenets of that spirituality would certainly have an impact on their understanding of vocation. A fourth reflection would encompass the notion of transcendence in relation to their religious beliefs. A research project conducted at Loyola University of Chicago gives insight into how religious faith affects the notion of vocation. Participants easily understood their call to religious ministry as emanating from a personal experience of God and relational intimacy. Educational administrators who have a strong faith tradition would certainly see their lives as an educational leader as complementary to their religious spirituality.[2]

A Method of Reflection

Reflection has taken many different approaches and is commonly referred to as meditation. Most, if not all, religions promote meditation as a means of understanding a person's spiritual relationship to the divine and for understanding the moral responsibilities that accompany a faith tradition. However, there are certain steps in the reflection process that are common to all methods and which can be adapted to either a faith tradition or other spiritualities. The call to reflection can be done in any setting and for any length of time during any part of the day because it is a mental process. However, the following steps could make the reflection process more productive.

- First, find a quiet place where you will not be disturbed and give yourself a few minutes of complete silence so that you can clear your mind of the requirements of the day.
- Second, try to be in touch with your feelings about the activities of the day. Are you happy, fearful, concerned, joyful, or uncomfortable with what occurred during the day?
- Third, consider if the activities of the day were in concert with your overall aspirations of being of service to the educational community.
- Fourth, consider how you should handle the activities of future days in order to live a more congruent life with your vocation as an educational leader.

Practical Discussions and Examples

Many preservice teachers set their goals toward educational leadership positions because of the prestige and higher salary that goes with these positions. It is not until a teacher has begun teaching that he or she can fully understand the vocational calling of an educator. That vocational calling must be a stronger incentive than any power or monetary incentive because a person will not serve as a strong leader without it. An educational leader who chooses the profession based on other issues than vocation can fall into disillusionment and dissatisfaction with his or her chosen field. An educational leader spends much of his or her time dealing with conflict resolution and problems/issues set in reality. While some educational leaders have internal good vision, the vision must also be set in reality in order to meet accomplishable goals.

The vocational calling includes not only wanting to educate children, but wanting to use managerial skills and communicative skills in a wider or broader way. An educational leader must be able to manage a school and staff, and at the same time, he or she must be able to communicate needs and conversations among various members of the learning community. An educational leader must be able to communicate with community leaders, parents, and stakeholders as well as staff, teachers, and students. An educational leader is serving a vocation because he or she is serving the people as a purpose for his or her life. Therefore, a leader must take into account the cultural community of the school and surrounding area as he or she makes appropriate choices in reality.

For example, principals should first look at the culture of the school and surrounding areas to see what values the school and community hold. These values are set in the reality that principals must ground themselves into while managing and creating mission and vision for the school. A principal who decides to focus on teacher retention in a transient area may not have the correct focus for that culture or reality. If a school is near a military base where children and teachers move in and out each year, and during the year, the principal would be better off serving his or her school by embracing change and creating curriculum and communication skills around change rather than serving in a traditional capacity where students mainly stay for an entire year and teachers stay for many years.

As with any professional, an educational leader must continually reflect and assess how he or she is doing in light of the situation, school, and learning community. Of course every person has good and bad days; every person sometimes wonders if they have made a correct career choice or decision; but an educational leader must really look deeply at his or her calling to make sure that he or she is happy with the choices made and the job done. If an administrator becomes disenfranchised, it may be time to move on, make changes, or reflect on other options. An educational leader is a public person serving those in a particular community. If his skills and values are better utilized in a different setting, then so be it. An educational leader must be able to embrace change as the school and culture continually evolves. Furthermore, an educational leader must serve the people's interests first.

Therefore, if a leader feels that a decision may positively affect the community, even if he or she is not in favor of that decision, he or she must think of others first. For example, suppose that a super-intendent of a small school district is at a state meeting where the idea of consolidation of his or her district and a neighboring district is discussed. This particular superintendent really believes in the value of small schools and what they can offer, in particular because he or she was educated in a small setting. However, suppose that he or she knows the high school students have limited choices regarding higher level courses and extra curricular opportunities; and he or she knows that consolidation would increase budgets and resources for these two things. He or she is correct in supporting the consolidation, despite his or her personal feelings, because of the greater good for his or her school and community.

A spiritual educational leader would also need to assess his or her vocational calling towards work in education. Many professions have strong individuals who do good things for the community. Doctors and health care professionals often say they enter the health profession to heal people. Business leaders and lawyers often work in not-for-profit entities, or donate money, time, or both to educa-tional and philanthropic areas. Educators are the same: many enter the profession because of the calling to help educate youth. Each profession may feel the need to defend itself as valuable, and those in education are not exempt. Continual reflection by the educational leader can help in explaining the vocational calling to education.

THE LEARNING COMMUNITY

In a learning community, an administrator shares responsibility for education with others, namely teachers, staff, parents, students, com-munity leaders, and other citizens.[3] Any community of learners is ultimately affected by individualism; therefore, learning takes place in both informal and formal settings. Students may have academic learning in the classroom, but they also learn much more in that class-room than academics. For example, students in an English class in high school may be learning about writing styles, but through conver-sation, they are also learning how to interact with each other and treat each other with respect. Therefore, learning communities offer places where both the actual curriculum and the hidden curriculum occur.

Spirituality

Since we are all unique and diverse individuals, each person brings characteristics of behavior, ideas, mannerisms, and spirituality. A person's character is typically framed his or her entire life and is affected by many things such as childhood upbringing, relationships, school, religion, spirituality, traditions, tragedy, and happiness. The thoughts and ideas of each individual are unique and are framed by experiences. Therefore, interactions between administrators, teachers, parents, and students always occur with differences in background and character. The diversity in what we are is what makes our educational system a wonderful learning opportunity for all involved. Problems arise only when things occur that are outside the realm of what is acceptable as an individual trait.

Suppose that two middle school children are playing on the playground. They are having a discussion about their families. One child describes the family vacation he is going to take this summer to Florida. The other describes that his family is too poor and can't take family vacations. The conversation can turn at this point based on how the students react to each other. A positive situation would be if the first child says, "Don't you ever go stay with your grandma or your aunt? Isn't that a vacation?" A negative situation would be if the first child begins to make fun of the other child because he is poor. The way children react is part of their spirituality that is being framed. If they believe that all people are innately good, then they may react with empathy and make the situation more positive. If they react poorly, then the conversation could turn into a problem, even escalating to physical violence between the children. Physical violence would be a situation that would be considered unacceptable despite what individual traits the children have.

Spirituality affects all members of the learning community. If the children take a field trip to the local firehouse and speak to fire fighters, they are again framing their own ideas and spirituality. They may see that these individuals fight fires and sometimes compromise their own lives in order to save others. They may learn that the firefighters are really doing jobs for the good of society. This positive influence frames a child's own spirituality. Likewise, if the students hear firefighters complain in a manner that indicates they are angry or disgruntled, then it frames the students' ideas of spirituality about people who work for the community. Without any intention, both the firefighters and the students would learn more about themselves and each other through conversation.

Spirituality and the Hidden Curriculum

All of the above examples can be considered the *hidden curriculum*. A hidden curriculum is a curriculum that is taught in school without lesson plans and not on purpose. It is learning that occurs as children are engaged in various situations where they learn things like respect for authority and time organization.[4] Much of what students will take with them from school into adulthood is what they learned in the hidden curriculum. In a learning community, all members continue to learn and grow merely through interactions and responsibilities to each other. Therefore, parents will learn and help their children discover appropriate ways to speak to others, respect for diversity, and so forth through the learning community.

Suppose two children playing on the playground are discussing angels, and one child says that angels are make-believe and the other child states that all good comes from angels who watch over people. These two children are having a conversation based on their own perspectives of spirituality. Who is right and who is wrong? The answer does not actually matter in this instance; what matters is that each child respects the other for her opinion, and it is equally important that each child has been affected by what the other says. Knowledge is power, and knowing what others believe will ultimately help frame what those small children will eventually believe as adults.

Dispositions of Spirituality

Spirituality can also be a part of the dispositions of adults in the school setting. That is, a person's spirituality is part of his or her character; therefore, dispositions are directly related to spirituality. All administrators, teachers, staff, and adults who interact with children must have appropriate dispositions in their dealings with children. What are dispositions and what dispositions must teachers and administrators possess in order to be effective role models?

Administrators hope that, with good judgment, they can hire individuals who would have learned how to teach and would know, from their own experiences, how to deal with different types of people easily. However, an effective leader would make sure that any person hired in the district would have a clear understanding of how to deal with others effectively. Dispositions are the ways in which a person works and interacts with others including both verbal and nonverbal communication. Dispositions embrace a large knowledge base that is modeled on the idea that each person must be treated with dignity and respect at all times. If educators want students to react positively towards others and work well together, then they must model it in every situation. This means being able to work with other educators despite personal negative thoughts about certain people, or professional thoughts of disagreement.

The Exponential Character of Learning and Spirituality

Learning is a lifelong process, and one in which every member of the learning community is affected by other members in the learning community. Character building continues for most members of the learning community—especially students. As stated previously, spirituality of others constantly affects character building merely by interactions and knowledge gained from those interactions with others. Learning can occur exponentially as members of the learning community interact with each other. The role of the educational administrator in this case is to be the leader in positive learning.

By example, educational leaders can model how to work with others, communicate effectively, interact with various community members, treat others with respect while valuing diversity, and provide a positive learning environment with a strong curriculum. By doing so, teachers, parents, and students will follow suit, thus allowing for an exponential effect of positive learning.

Synthesis Versus Analysis of Knowledge and Spirituality

Through acquiring knowledge, all members of the learning community must clarify the difference between synthesis of knowledge and analysis of knowledge. As explained previously, every individual is shaped and framed somewhat by spirituality, and each individual is affected through interactions with others. As individuals learn from each other, each individual must first synthesize the knowledge and then analyze it. For instance, take into consideration the above mentioned example of the two small children on the playground talking about angels. First, the children must synthesize what they are hearing since it is new for them. They must list both aspects of angels, and maybe even ask others about their opinions on angels. Then, each person must individually analyze whether they believe the information is true, is not true, or could be true. Synthesis can be done jointly, but analysis is done individually since the outcome of the analysis ultimately affects the character and thoughts of that individual.

The Critical Thinking Mandate and Spirituality

In synthesis and analysis, an individual is engaging in critical thinking—a process that educational leaders want of all students.
One role of the educational leader is to understand the differences between student output and teacher input. Research is one tool to clearly define teacher input and clearly assess student output.

By the nature of educational leader positions, administrators are in a position of power. How they use this power is the key to leading well and using spirituality. Since many administrators chose their work as a vocation or sense of calling, they must never lose sight of the reasons they are in the school systems in the first place. Their jobs exist around the need to provide quality education for children, and good resources and a positive learning environment for the entire learning community.

The media has educated many community members about the inappropriate behaviors or bad decisions of some very powerful people in education, politics, and business in recent years. It appears that many people gain too much power and lose sight of responsibilities, thinking they are not touchable. As educational leaders, it is imperative that good judgment leads to appropriate decisions and the appropriate use of power.

Power should not be thought of in an authoritarian way, but in a leadership way. Good leadership and decision making makes the issue of power moot. A classic thought is that those who are good leaders do not need to remind people of their power; those who constantly favor power as a resource need help in leadership.

Assessment and Spirituality

All dimensions of the educational leadership enterprise are subject to assessment, and there is no doubt that assessment is paramount in the minds of all educators, parents, politicians, and the general public. These groups' interests in assessment vary widely, but all of them understand that assessment is an expectation and the responsibility of educational leaders. Superintendents and principals are specifically charged with this responsibility.

There are three types of assessment. The first is the assessment of event issues such as the time and place of staff development programs or assessing a new strategy for teaching reading. The time of day and the quality of the environment for testing students is an example of this first type of assessment. It is easy to conduct this type of assessment of those who are involved through a survey instrument, interviews, or focus groups.

The second type of assessment concerns the objectives attainment of programs, processes, and procedures for all members of the school and school district communities. Thus, assessment of the effectiveness of the professional negotiations process or the mathematics curriculum are examples of objectives attainment assessment. This type of assessment is also implemented through both quantitative and qualitative techniques such as surveys, interviews, and focus groups. However, other assessments can also be used in the statistical analysis of students' test data, and the implementation of a collective bargain agreement can be assessed through the number of grievances that were filed by the parities to the agreement.

The final area of assessment is impact, which is rather difficult to assess and is generally demonstrated through narratives about how the programs have affected the perceptions, attitudes, and opinions of educators, parents, politicians, and the general public. The assessment of impact usually involves cultural analysis that was presented in Chapter 2.

The point in this section is that even the spiritual dimension of educational leadership requires assessment techniques because it is only within the reality of given situations that the spiritual vocation of leaders can be carried out.

Practical Discussions and Examples

Students learn a great deal in school. They learn from teachers, administrators, support staff, custodians, coaches, and each other. Every communication event and every aspect of every school day is a chance for learning. School is the practice for children to interact and communicate effectively as they transition from children to adults. Therefore, the importance of interactions and school climate is crucial. An educational leader, by nature, strongly sets the tone for interaction and climate in a school. A leader who is friendly, walking the halls, interacting with students, parents, and teachers, and who generally makes himself or herself approachable and visible automatically encourages a more positive school culture and climate. An educational leader should encourage appropriate conversations and interactions among staff and children. For example, if a child sees a principal speaking inappropriately to a parent at the school, the child may think that since adults speak that way to each other, children can also. Furthermore, the child may be afraid to speak to the principal and be afraid for her parent to come to the school. Therefore, spirituality, dispositions, and the hidden curriculum are intertwined.

Regarding assessment, it is crucial that educational leaders continually regard assessment as they do reflection. Documented assessment is the key to showing students, parents, and stakeholders facts about the school or learning taking place. Because a principal and teachers are held accountable for student learning, careful documentation is a necessity. Assessment of student, parents, and stakeholder views is also important because of the impact of school culture. Again, an educational leader must put aside her own biases and views if the assessment shows different attitudes or values from the school community. For example, suppose that Rainbow Elementary School always has a carnival near the end of the year after the state mandated testing has been completed. The principal, feeling pressure from the Board of Education to focus only on academics and test scores, decides to eliminate the carnival this year and, instead, concentrate solely on academics for the remainder of the year. A group of parents expresses dissatisfaction with the decision, so the principal surveys the teachers and an advisory group of parents, and discovers that while they all feel academics is important, they feel that a celebration is equally important. Therefore, while the principal may not like the celebration, she should consider the impact of canceling—would it improve academics or negatively affect school culture? Therefore, assessment is important in many ways, and decisions made without appropriate assessment can also affect the spirituality and curriculum in the school.

THE IMPORTANCE OF RESEARCH

Most, if not all, spiritual ideas are knowable as intuitions rather than through direct experiences. As a consequence, researching the spiritual must be conducted on experiences that are evidentiary in support of intuitions. Evidence can be qualitative or quantitative; thus a focus group, interview, or survey can be utilized to investigate the perceptions of teachers about the relevance of a staff development workshop on how to teach English to immigrant children who utilize English as their second language. This same situation allows the educational administrator to also investigate the perceptions and attitudes of teachers on the social justice issues surrounding immigration. As interpreted by the research, those perceptions can serve as evidence of teachers' interiorization of the importance of the humane treatment of children who are immigrants. Thus the research is centered on the notion of interiority.

Every educational leader is responsible for using research to aid in decision making.[5] Therefore, the educational leader must be prepared and ready to conduct research. How is research collected and used in schools, and how is it related to spirituality and vocation?

Research should be collected on programs that schools offer, on student achievement, and on teacher or support staff interventions with students. All research should be used in order to make decisions for the future of a particular program in the school, for the assessment of student achievement, or for interventions that faculty members are trying. If educators want the best for all students, then it is necessary to perform a critical analysis of the learning community and its actions.

Spirituality affects what teachers and educational leaders believe should be happening in schools. Since spirituality affects vocation, educational leaders are always trying to offer the best options for students to help them grow and succeed. For example, suppose that a new educational leader in a school wants to try a peer tutoring and counseling program for teenagers. After the first year, the administrator should provide some sort of assessment and research on this program. Even though everyone's intentions are good, and the idea is based in spirituality and human kindness, evaluation is crucial to see the direction in which the program should grow or change.

Thus it should be obvious that assessment data and information can also be used to research the concept of vocation. The statistical treatment of data and qualitative analyses can produce an ongoing clarification and understanding of the assumptions and epistemology upon which the project was constructed. Thus the gathering of facts (information), the correlation of information (knowledge), and the interpretation and application of knowledge (understanding) can be used for multiple purposes.

Practical Discussions and Examples

Research is a crucial part of the job of an educational leader. Decisions can be made and supported with documentation. Furthermore, a leader is only as good as those around him. Therefore, a good leader will utilize her staff to the best of their abilities, and ask for opinions and suggestions as educational professionals from them. Empowerment is a key to a positive school culture, and empowering teachers, staff, and students by engaging them in conversation that ultimately leads to decision making creates a good environment.

Since spirituality affects the vocations of all educators, ideas expressed in a school are always for the growth of children. However, even if an idea is good, the product may not be what was anticipated, and assessment and evaluation is important in order to make decisions. For example, suppose that one team of fifth grade teachers wants to start a "buddy" program, and this program is to encourage academic improvement in second graders. Therefore, a fifth grader is paired up to a second grader, and tutoring/academic time is devoted each week for the pair. Suppose when assessments are made at the end of the year, little academic improvement was shown. This is a way to change the focus of the program. Assessment also diverts blame. It isn't the *fault* of the team that the program did not have the outcome they anticipated. It would be true that academics did not improve, but maybe social and communication skills improved for both the second and fifth graders. Therefore, the focus of the program could be shifted with the knowledge from the assessment.

SUMMARY

First, the authors described the vocational calling for educational leaders. This vocation is based in spirituality and the purpose of serving the public by educating children. This vocation is based in the following assumptions: reality, personal integrity development, spirituality, and reasons for choosing educational leadership. Next, the content and method of reflection are discussed. Educational leaders *must* continually reflect in their work to make sure that they are making appropriate decisions for their particular school cultures and environments. Next, spirituality is discussed in the context of the learning community, the hidden curriculum, dispositions, character of learning, synthesis and analysis of knowledge, critical thinking, and assessment. Finally, the importance of research in spirituality and decision making is discussed. Every school culture is different, and an effective educational leader uses assessment and evaluation as he or she engages in the decision-making process.

ILLUSTRATION: A CASE OF VOCATION AND DISPOSITIONS

The Setting

Bollingbrook, Connecticut, is an affluent suburb of New York City and is quite far removed from the center of the city. Most of the families that live in Bollingbrook are from the upper economic class. Many of the families have two parents who are professionals, and a number of the parents are doctors and lawyers, with one parent commuting into New York City daily. It is one of the most expensive places to live in Connecticut, with many homes selling in the one-to-three-million-dollar range. A number of the children in this area go to private schools, but there is also a very good public school option. Teachers are well educated, and average teacher and administrator salaries are higher in this district than in any other district in the state.

Bollingbrook Middle School is a newly constructed building where approximately six hundred students attend Grades 6–8. The majority of the students are Caucasian, Indian, and Asian. The facilities are state-of-the-art due to the large tax base that the community provides. There are three fully equipped computer labs, and one is also a multimedia resource lab. Each classroom uses SMART board technology, and there are two portable laptop classrooms that teachers are free to use. The student-to-teacher ratio is approximately fifteen to one, and most teachers do not leave the school once they are hired. The average number of years of experience of the teachers is fifteen. The average teacher salary is $68,000, and the average administrator salary in the district is $100,000. Almost all teachers have a master's degree in their field or in teaching, and all administrators hold doctorate degrees.

The families generally are considered to have high moral codes and work ethics. Most children are expected to do well in school and work hard. Likewise, the parents are fairly demanding but supportive. The school has parental help in organizing activities, fundraisers, and getting involved in student work and life. Parents regularly communicate with teachers about student success and problems, and teachers typically give their home and school phone numbers to parents to use at their discretion. Teachers are generally very intelligent and professional, offering stimulating classes and curriculum for the students.

The Situation

A popular topic in schools including Bollingbrook is that of dispositions. For many years, administrators have assumed that they would hire good, wholesome people who would know how to interact with children, parents, and the community. However, this has not always been the case. New and veteran teachers are questioned about their abilities to deal with these different people in an appropriate way. An administrator is ultimately responsible for the actions of teachers in a school, whether it is supporting a teacher's actions or taking alternative means to reprimand a teacher who has acted inappropriately. Both situations require an administrator to have a clear idea about what dispositions his or her teachers must possess; furthermore, he or she must make clear to teachers what dispositions are necessary.

Dr. Jackson has been the principal at Bollingbrook for fifteen years. She has discussed regularly with teachers their vocation: the call to be a professional educator to children. She is proud of her teachers and staff, who are excellent educators and always address parents and students in a professional manner. She has led workshops on professionalism, including topics such as relationships with students, relationships with teachers, appropriate dress, appropriate language, and appropriate interactions with each other. She considers herself an expert in conflict resolution and has indeed been a great manager of people in her school.

Spirituality

The National Council for Accreditation of Teacher Education sets performance-based standards for the preparation of teachers and other professional school personnel. The standards require that candidates demonstrate knowledge, skills, and professional dispositions necessary to help all students learn. These dispositions are not specified, but can relate to areas of care for children; instilling respect among class members; working professionally and well with other adults including teachers, teacher aides, and administrators; and reflecting on one's own actions and management skills. Therefore, it is imperative that administrators clearly observe and discuss with teachers which dispositions are appropriate and which are not. Spirituality affects dispositions because spirituality includes topics such as ethical behavior, moral values, and "right vs. wrong." These are all issues that affect the way in which a teacher behaves, teaches, and interacts with various members of the community, parents, and children. Dr. Jackson has not specifically ever had to deal with major problems regarding dispositions from her teachers. It is a culture that is understood by her teachers and community that everyone is professional and treats each other with obvious respect.

The Problem

A new teacher, Mr. Stephens, has been hired at Bollingbrook Middle School. He comes from a nearby district with good references and a great education and teaching background. He seems to be doing a good job; however, soon after school begins a parent in the district calls and asks to speak to Dr. Jackson so that she can discuss the conduct of her child's teacher. It appears to the parent that Mr. Stephens has been making inappropriate comments about her daughter's clothes. She further states that the teacher is dressing provocatively and is becoming "too friendly" to the students. When asked what "provocatively" means, the parent states that the teacher is constantly wearing his shirt unbuttoned too far. Since this is the first complaint against Mr. Stephens, the principal decides she will quietly investigate and then call the parent back. Dr. Jackson is aware that in a nearby school district, a teacher was recently let go for suspicion of sexual misconduct with a student. She wonders if this has affected the situation in her school. When the principal approaches the classroom, she notices that Mr. Stephens is wearing a button-down shirt with the top four buttons not fastened and relatively tight pants. He is talking in a friendly manner with the students, but appears to be professional. After class, the principal enters the classroom to inquire about Mr. Stephens' teaching style and methods with the children. She refers to the parent's comments. Mr. Stephens takes offense at the comments, and states that he is an excellent teacher and that his dress has no impact on his teaching ability.

The principal worries that personally engaging in this conversation further could cross the lines of sexual harassment—in particular because she is an older female and Mr. Stephens is a young, new male teacher in the school. She decides to ask both a male and female veteran teacher to help her talk with the new teacher later in the week. She and the other teachers approach the situation using the issue of dispositions with the teacher.

Discernment Questions

1. What dispositions should Dr. Jackson discuss with Mr. Stephens?

2. What issues of sexual harassment is Dr. Jackson afraid of?

3. Should Dr. Jackson do anything more about this situation?

4. How do her own ideas about vocation affect her perception of Mr. Stephens?

5. How does vocation enter the conversation with regards to the manner in which the teacher might relate to the community?

6. How do dispositions affect the teacher and the administrator in relation to the learning community?

7. How is spirituality related to vocation and disposition in this case?

Conversations About the Case Study

Dr. Jackson was right to investigate the parent complaint, especially if she suspects that parents have heightened awareness about conduct in the school because of the nearby school district lawsuit. However, it may have been easier for Dr. Jackson to approach the teacher about the parent comment after school when they would both have more time to talk about it. Dr. Jackson should be prepared to discuss dress codes or issues of disposition at that time, and quite possibly it would be better to do this with all new teachers. Even if Dr. Jackson thinks his dress is fine (although borderline), Mr. Stephens needs to think about whether he wants to take on this battle. It may be easier to dress a bit more professionally, and it could solve the problem (if there is one) or future problems. If Mr. Stephens is passionate about teaching and really is an excellent teacher, then he may be wiser to do things that allow others to focus on his teaching.

Dr. Jackson should not be scared of sexual harassment. What she should do is take a valid assessment of any dress code issues for all teachers in the building. Next, in a professional way, she should address those issues to all involved. This manner includes direct and honest conversations about dispositions and the impression that teachers have on children, their parents, and this particular community. If the teachers in the building are all professional and truly believe in their vocation to serve the students and community, then they should not have an issue with appropriately requested dress code changes. Dr. Jackson must be consistent in these changes, require them for both men and women, and allow freedom of choice for teachers as long as it would not be a problem for the learning community. Any administrator knows that the more proactive one is ahead of time, the fewer problems unfold and escalate. One way to have avoided the entire situation is to have a veteran mentor teacher assigned to Mr. Stephens upon his arrival at the school and to have an orientation agenda that includes the issue of dispositions.

EXERCISE:
ASSESSMENT, COMMUNICATION, AND REFLECTION

Based on your professional experience and knowledge, describe how you could use teacher empowerment, assessment, communication, and reflection in the following situations:

Establishing a vision or mission for the school

_____

_____

_____

Developing a curriculum scope and sequence plan for seventh- and eighth-grade science

_____

_____

_____

Creating a student behavioral code and a teacher/staff behavioral code

_____

_____

_____

Developing a school-community relations program

_____

_____

_____

Creating an event policies and procedures plan

_____

_____

_____

Creating student assessment policies

_____

_____

_____

Implementation of a new extra curricular music program

_____

_____

_____

The development of a parent advisory group and student advisory group

_____

_____

_____

CHAPTER FOUR

The Practice of Educational Leadership From Experience, Reflection, and Beliefs

CHAPTER OBJECTIVES

- To explore the dimensions of transcendental leadership in order to clarify the spiritual bases of educational leadership
- To explain how the dimensions of transcendental leadership are supportive of best practice in educational leadership
- To explain how school and school district cultures can enhance the spiritual bases of educational leadership
- To explain how cultural analysis can be implemented and used to support the spiritual bases of educational leadership

THE RATIONALE FOR SPIRITUAL LEADERSHIP

There are several reasons why this chapter has been developed for this book on spirituality. First, the current state of affairs in both the superintendency and principalship has prompted the need to consider a different approach to leadership. These affairs are signs of the times and can be exemplified as follows:

- The milieu within which the superintendent of schools and building principals function is very complex, ambiguous, and stressful.
- Superintendents and principals are required to perform their responsibilities even though they may not have job security.
- Boards of education continue to cross over the line between governance and administration.
- The superintendency and principalship are becoming more political.

Further, teachers, superintendents, and principals are sometimes blamed for the poor performance of students and for a lack of financial stewardship. Some criticisms may be legitimate, but in general educators are doing an excellent job in most schools and school districts. Also, most educators are supportive of educational reform and advocate for equal educational opportunity for all children as a means of creating a just society. However, it is rather difficult for most educators to find adequate spiritual leadership theories that will help direct their professional responsibilities to their schools, school districts, and the educational community at large.

The record indicates that some superintendents and principals fail within the first few years of being an administrator because of the extreme pressures that are placed on them as they carry out their responsibilities. Even so, there are still many people willing to assume administrator positions when they are vacated.

As set forth in the previous chapter, a major issue in the lives of many administrators is the search for purpose that transcends the paycheck and prestige that comes from being an educational administrator. Thus this chapter presents a model theory of leadership that could fill the gap for many administrators in their search for meaning in relation to being an educational leader. That theory is Transcendental Leadership.

Transcendence refers to living a life dedicated to leadership within and on behalf of the academic community and profession in contrast with finding an administrative position in order to just make a living. Without a sense of transcendency, many principals and superintendents may overlook the reason why they became educators in the beginning of their careers. Thus there is a need for many administrators to practice focused reflection, which was set forth in Chapter 3.[1]

TRANSCENDENTAL LEADERSHIP

Transcendental educational leadership requires a person to undertake a lifelong process of discerning how he or she can be of service to the academic community and profession. Further, carrying out his or her responsibilities as a superintendent or principal is the arena within which he or she will develop the transcendental perspective. This sense of service is difficult to sustain unless a person has an agenda to be followed. Operating from such a theoretical base insures that a person will develop a spiritual approach to educational leadership.

In choosing or developing a theoretical base, superintendents and principals must be open to the cultural differences that exist between the people they serve, and they must recognize that the religious and philosophical values of other people can have a profound effect upon their leadership style.[2]

This understanding of the cultural implications of leadership is of particular importance because of the immigration that has taken place in the United States over the last two decades. It has created a new challenge for superintendents and principals in terms of enculturation. The new immigrants have brought to our shores a new "georeligious" perspective. There are now significant numbers of second generation Buddhists, Hindus, Jains, Muslims, and Sikhs living in the United States. Obviously, these religions are held by people who are not from Eastern and Western Europe; rather, they are Cambodian, Chinese, Filipino, Japanese, Korean, Thai, and Vietnamese.[3]

However, there are significant numbers of Hispanics and African Americans who have religious beliefs similar to those of Eastern and Western Europe. Such diversity requires dialogue with educators and the members of these religions and ethic groups. It is only through dialogue and discourse that true understanding can be reached. Of course, the purpose of such dialogue and discourse is not to compromise beliefs; rather, it should be an attempt to examine and explain values. People from every generation seek a relationship with something beyond their own personal existence. However, spirituality is not easily grasped and exists as a vague notion in the minds of many educational leaders.

Practical Discussions and Examples

An educational leader will encounter multiple children, parents, and members of the community who hold different views in many areas. One of these will be the difference in religion. For example, some rural principals may feel at ease because the majority of his or her children come from Catholic or Protestant backgrounds. What happens when a new family moves to town and practices the Hindu faith? A principal must examine what options are available in this small school or district to those new students. For example, the principal, after discussion with the parents, realizes that the children do not eat meat. The principal must make sure that the school lunch provided has alternatives to meat that are healthy and adequate for the family. Suppose that the physical education curriculum has always included a two week lesson in dance, and this family also explains that they would prefer that their daughter not partake in the dance lesson because of religious reasons. What kinds of expectations should the principal have, and what kinds of alternatives can be made available for the children?

The principal can also use these types of situations as educational opportunities. Instead of making only alternative arrangements for the child, the principal could ask if the child feels comfortable enough to explain to others why she doesn't partake in the school dance program, and what activities her family may do instead. This kind of opportunity educates all involved, and as stated previously, what the principal may hear could change his or her own ideas about what types of physical education activities should be offered. Understanding of various religious beliefs will only help the educational leader in understanding the different backgrounds and cultures his students come from. Armed with this knowledge, the principal can make the most appropriate day-to-day decisions to best suit the students.

Spiritual Leadership Paradigm and Elements[4]

The basic premise of spiritual leadership is that an educational leader acts from the totality of who he or she is as a human being. Also, educational leaders are usually cognizant of the fact that their decisions are influenced by more that just the immediate circumstances. Further, they generally understand that the effects of their decisions can have an impact that goes beyond the present situation. Consequently, it is necessary to consider how spiritual leadership is operationalized.

Operationalization is a process that includes various elements that are activated in order to guarantee that a given leadership theory is properly practiced. Many different theories have similar elements, but it is the combination of elements and the disposition of the person using a theory that makes it effective. There are six manifestations of the spiritual approach: (1) utilizes a reflection paradigm, (2) practices the principle of subsidiarity, (3) acts from a political base, (4) acts from a sense of duty, (5) advocates social justice, and (6) formulates professional positions through discourse.

Utilizes a Reflection Paradigm[5]

The first manifestation of spiritual leadership concerns the constant need to reflect on the decision-making process, which is the primary task of an educational leader. It is the one responsibility that defines the role and function of educational leadership. Superintendents and principals are constantly called upon to make decisions. Chapters 1 and 3 deal with the reflection responsibility in greater depth than is presented here. However, it is important is touch on a few points at this juncture in spiritual leadership.

All reflection begins with a consideration of what an educational leader is confronted with in carrying out his or her responsibilities. Leadership cannot be a top-down phenomenon but rather must begin with what is taking place in the classrooms, corridors, cafeteria, media center, parking lots, and playgrounds. Finally, it means knowing and understanding the attitudes, emotions, opinions, and values of all stakeholders: parents, students, teachers, staff members, administrators, and the public at large.

It is from this base that school administrators can ascertain if what they believe in terms of educational theory really works. There is no question about the value and importance of educational theory. Practice without theory is chaos. Educational leadership theory, however, is based on a personal system of spiritual values and beliefs.

There is another important aspect to this spiritual reflection paradigm. It is the reciprocal relationship that exists between practice, theory, and spirituality. Not only does everything begin with practice but in fact, practice can change theory which, in turn, can change a superintendent's and principal's spirituality. Such a change in spirituality can further alter a person's leadership theory that ultimately could affect his or her practice.

Practices the Principle of Subsidiarity[6]

The second manifestation is the principle of subsidiarity, which has a unique history. It originated in the disciplines of social ethics and social economics. The principle basically states that decisions should be made at the lowest possible level in a given organization. There is no question as to the relevance of allowing teachers and staff members to do their jobs without interference from administrators. There is also no question about the firsthand knowledge and experience that teachers and staff members have that makes them eminently more qualified to handle issues and problems.

The application of this principle empowers teachers and staff members as they carry out the responsibilities of their respective positions. Thus, decisions about budgeting, curriculum development, maintenance of facilities, public relations activities, technology implementation, and so forth are shared responsibilities. Essentially, the superintendent becomes a consultant and mentor to assistant superintendents, directors, and principals; the principal becomes a consultant and mentor to teachers and other staff members.

Further, the mentor responsibility of the superintendent or principal is sometimes adaptive rather than technical. He or she must help others recognize how their values influence their behaviors in the face of new realities.

Practical Discussions and Examples

Excellent educators are those who constantly reflect on each day and make changes accordingly. Educational leaders expect their best teachers to reflect and make changes to lessons for children, and they should not expect any less of themselves. Each interaction or decision should be reflected upon so that the educational leader can continue to make the correct decisions for those he or she is serving.

For example, suppose that the superintendent must make a decision concerning when spring break should occur in the district. The community he serves was traditionally Catholic, so the district spring break had always been held during Easter. Because the date of Easter changes yearly, the spring break changed accordingly. However, over the past five years, the superintendent has seen an influx of Jewish students; therefore, he thinks it might be a good idea to place the spring break around Passover. When he moves the spring break that year, many people in his community are upset that it was changed without input. Furthermore, some parents claim that it wasn't fair that the superintendent was creating the schedule for one particular religion. By trying to please many people, the superintendent has caused possibly equally as many people to be upset. Therefore, the superintendent must reflect on the decision made—who does it serve, and does it serve his community of students and parents well? Maybe in the future he should let a vote of parents and teachers decide. Using the principle of subsidiarity, he should take the teachers' advice as they know the students best. They can inform the principal of how it may affect the students, and they could vote, and the majority vote could justify the decision. Or, if decisions about spring break are equally split, then he could set the break according to the semester calendar and keep it the same each year despite whether it falls over a religious holiday at all. But most important, he should develop a plan of action based on reflection of the situation, taking into account what his teachers say.

Acts From a Political Base[7]

The third manifestation is concerned with how educational leaders attempt to manage the impact that their actions and decisions will have on the actions and decisions of others and on institutions. The conceptualization of what constitutes a political base can be understood in a series of tensions.

- The first tension concerns the responsibilities of the national government in relation to the responsibilities of the state government. The role and function of superintendents, principals, and other administrators in this arena is to lead the school district or school so that there is no confusion on the part of parents, students, teachers, staff members, other administrators, and the general public about the responsibilities of both federal and state governmental agencies.
- The second tension deals with the rights of the national government in relation to the rights of the individual. The role and function of administrators is to ensure that the rights of individual students, parents, teachers, staff members, and so forth are not in conflict with the rights of the national government.
- The third tension involves the rights of the state government in relation to the rights of the individual. Thus, funding from the state for gifted programs must not set aside the rights of other students to a quality education through significant depletion of the general pool of money available for education.
- The fourth tension concerns Constitutional rights in relation to ethical rights. It may be constitutional to expel a student for having an illegal drug at school, but it might be an ethical issue if the school district does not provide an alternative educational program for such students.

- The fifth tension involves the rights of the general public in relation to the rights of special interest groups, which tends to be a problem for superintendents, principals, and boards of education. It is the responsibility of educational leaders to strike a balance between the rights of both the general public and advocates.
- The last tension regards the rights of the marginalized in relation to the influence of the decision makers. There is no question about the great influx of immigrants into some school districts. These people generally are not the decision makers in most school districts and their plight can often be overlooked.

Acts From a Sense of Duty

Everyone has a multitude of duties that are sometimes ambiguous to identify, but generally can be classified into the following: duties toward family, friends, colleagues, neighbors, acquaintances, and oneself; and duties toward a person's employer, other employees, and the profession.

The philosophy of Aristotle speaks to the duty of citizens and is contained in his *Politics*. The purpose of the state is the fostering of the supreme good. In his approach to the good, Aristotle viewed the natural end of a person to be the good life and thus, the state must be a natural society. A key to Aristotle's philosophy is his idea that citizens are both rulers and subjects vested with the right to participate in making laws and the right to participate in the administration of justice.[8] He also raised the question as to the relationship between the virtues of a good person and the virtues of a good citizen. According to Aristotle, the virtues may intersect, but the virtues of those who govern are different from those of the citizen. However, in relation to the tenet of governing, the person who has never learned how to obey cannot know how to command. Thus, the virtues of a good citizen resides in his or her knowing how to do both, govern and be governed.[9]

Marcus Aurelius Antoninus is a second resource person from the classical period in history who has had deep insight into the human condition in relation to duty. He wrote the *Meditations* to expound on the unseen powers behind creation, on the purpose and nature of human existence, and on how people should live their lives. He was a dutiful person, and the perspectives he shared were driven by his experience as a civil leader. For Marcus, destiny is synonymous with duty, which signals that a person may not have the luxury of deciding his or her duty, but may have it thrust upon himself or herself. His basic principle appears to be that experiencing life will give a person self-control and courage in the pursuit of truth and justice. The tool for this pursuit is reason. If a person channels his or her zeal and energy with truthfulness toward fulfilling his or her duty, no other power will be able to divert him or her from this purpose. It is through reason that people are capable of establishing universal laws of conduct, which is the common bond that unites all people in the pursuit of goodness. The *Meditations* also address the perennial enigma of why bad things happen to good people and why good things happen to bad people. Marcus held the position that nature makes no distinction between good and bad people when bestowing pain or pleasure, life or death, fame or dishonor. Thus people should live their lives with the same indifference and perform their duty without regard to their condition.[10]

The third source that speaks pointedly to educational leadership is John Dewey's pragmatism. Many school practices are attributed directly to him, and Dewey's influence continues to be felt in contemporary education. Dewey considered the psychological and social dimensions of child growth and development as important aspects of the learning-instructional process. He further recognized the importance of the cultural context of education and the need to transmit the fundamental principles of American democracy in schools. Further, he called for the active participation of students in school because they need to assume leadership roles in order to understand the requirements of citizenship. Further, the rights of minorities must not be nullified through the rule of the majority. Change is supported by Dewey through his belief that truth is relative to time and place. In relation to student discipline, he advocated for a permissive approach.

Dewey believed that education was a lifelong process and that instruction should be developed along thematic and problem solving bases. One of the most important implications for educational leadership coming forth from Dewey's philosophy is the need for empowerment of parents, students, teachers, staff members, and administrators. Teacher empowerment calls for them to be active participants in the decision-making process about policy and procedural issues that affect the entire school organization. Further, teacher empowerment means providing them with the means and opportunity to solve their own problems, to make short and long term plans, and to direct their own growth and development.

The empowerment of students has some of the same elements as the empowerment of teachers. Student empowerment emanates from a school culture that promotes an intense focus on students, flexibility and resourcefulness, risk taking and experimentation. A school culture that considers students as team members rather than as the products of the educational enterprise is the attitude that will permit the empowerment of students. In order to be active members of the school community, student must be given the opportunity to develop problem-solving and leadership skills. True student empowerment will be ineffective unless such empowerment opportunities are extended to students with disabilities and to those students who do not fit the mainstream model.[11]

Advocates Social Justice[12]

Social justice is the spiritual guide that regulates how people live out their lives as members of a given community. The substance of justice is entitlement that refers to those rights to which individuals and groups of people have a claim. The responsibilities of society to the individual are referred to as distributive justice. The responsibilities of each person to society are termed legal justice. Commutative justice involves those responsibilities that exist between individuals. Justice also involves restitution, which is the rights of a person to have an entitlement restored, which was previously withheld.

Contractarianism is a political philosophy which sets forth the notion that society should be designed by the very people who will live in it. Thus government comes into existence through a contract or agreement among the people to be governed.

John Rawls is a contemporary contractarian. He describes his theory of justice in terms of fairness. His basic premise is that the best principles of justice for the basic structure of any society are those that would be the object of an original agreement in the establishment of a society. These principles would be derived by free rational people as an initial position of equality. Rawls elucidated two principles that he believed people would choose in the initial situation in order to implement the notion of fairness. The first principle asserts that each person is to have an equal right to a system of liberties that is compatible with a similar system of liberties available to all people. The second principle asserts that social and economic inequalities must benefit the least advantaged, and that equal opportunity to secure offices and positions must be open to all. In explaining how present inequities may benefit the least advantaged, he developed the principle of just savings.

Formulates Professional Positions Through Discourse[13]

This is the final manifestation of the elements in spiritual transcendental leadership. Implementing the pluralistic point of view in educational leadership is not only a spiritual but also a political issue because public school districts are state agencies, which are also impacted by federal laws and agencies. Jürgen Habermas is a contemporary philosopher who views public discourse as the pursuit of how conflicting interests can result in appropriate judgments. Embedded within his theoretical design is a procedure for human argumentation that is reasoned agreement by those who will be affected by the norm. The central principle of public discourse is that the validity of a norm rests on the acceptability of the consequences of the norm by all participants in the practical discourse. This is a shift from the solitary individual to the community of subjects in dialogue. Making a decision about the fairness of a norm cannot take place only in the minds of administrators, but must be played out in actual discourse with other people. In Habermas's model, each person must be willing and able to appreciate the perspective of other people.

Public discourse is difficult to implement. Habermas perceives the overarching problem to be isolation in contemporary society. He believes that the role of the philosopher in society is to mediate and facilitate a framework within which people can communicate in a nondefensive manner. Thus communication can lead to influencing based on reason rather than on coercion. Further, the reasoned validity which people elucidate in discourse tends to transcend the present context and sets the stage for future discourse.

Habermas's principle of universalization is operationalized within the context of a discourse that emanates from a reasoned position. Thus reasoning is the basis of all discourse and participants must agree to this rationality. Participants should be free from external and internal coercion other than the force of the best argument, which at that point supports the cooperative search for truth. Because of the limitations of time and space, it is necessary to institutionalize discourse; the topics to be discussed and the contributions of participants must be organized in terms of opening, adjournment, and resumption of discussion.

Discourse can be effective only if it is applied to questions that can be dealt with through impartial judgment. This implies that the process will lead to an answer equally beneficial to all stakeholders. This does not mean that discourse seeks to reach consensus, but rather to generate convictions in the participants. Further, Habermas sees the degree to which a society, its institutions, its political culture, its traditions, and its everyday practices permit a noncoercive and nonauthoritarian form of spiritual living as the hallmark of rational morality that is derived from discourse. Developing a working knowledge and understanding of pluralism, justice, and discourse will certainly lead to more spiritual-laden resolution of conflicts.[14]

Practical Discussions and Example

Educational leaders must advocate for all children as their sense of duty, providing the best educational opportunity for all. For some educational leaders, this goal becomes one that dictates their daily decision making and their long-term plans, and is the focus for their entire career. Suppose that a superintendent takes a new job in a lower socioeconomic district that has seen the largest influx of new immigrants to a metro area in the last five years. Most of the students she encounters were born abroad and immigrated to the United

States at school age. Therefore, while there is a large English language learner (ELL) population and language continues to be a focus for her schools, an equally difficult situation includes the parents of these children. They do not have the language to voice opinions to educational leaders. While most were highly educated in their home country, they left professional jobs to immigrate to the United States and currently work minimum wage jobs as they try to rebuild a life here. Many work long hours and do not feel they know the United States educational system well enough to get involved or ask questions. What sense of duty does this superintendent have to these children and their families? How can she help empower both the students and parents?

Starting with the principle of subsidiarity, the superintendent needs to talk with children and teachers in buildings. Many of the children are the interpreters for their parents; thus, to reach parents, administrators may need to channel much information through students. It is crucial that these students do not get lost because their parents cannot be vocal advocates for them. These children and parents need to be part of the decision making in the school because those decisions affect so many children and families like them. The school may need to alter budgets to include many translators at school events, and to offer family activities or community activities at various times of the day and weekends to accommodate a range of working schedules. The school district may even try to offer free English lessons for parents interested. Being open and showing that parental input is valuable is a first step in making both the children and parents welcome to the school. By organizing parent organizations and empowering parents to become involved, more and more parents in the community will contribute to the education of the children in that community. It may be easier to begin by forming a student group that is responsible for some decisions in the school, like field trips or extra curricular activities. If children are the translators for families, then empowering them first may help achieve empowerment of parents who can ultimately become decision makers by serving on boards of education or working in the school. An educational leader must find a way to make these things happen in her given situation.

CULTURE

School is a culture in itself, and it is affected by the individual cultures that students bring and the community culture of which it is a part. As is the case with most cultures, schools have their own traditions, rituals, routines, rewards, punishments, times, classrooms, and so forth.[15] Culture is constantly challenged as new situations arise. But the culture continues to set the tone for the school day and helps determine activities and courses that are offered as part of the school system.

Components of Culture

There are many definitions of culture, and no one definition can encompass all of its aspects.[16] However, culture is delineated in a school by many things: attitudes, beliefs, values, opinions, and feelings. These are all affected by one's spirituality. Someone's attitudes and beliefs are framed from previous experience and exposure, and this affects how schools operate as cultures are brought together. Opinions are framed by attitudes, beliefs, and feelings of an administrator or school staff, and sometimes these opinions are right and sometimes wrong. All of these affect communication, activities, and behavior in a school. Therefore, it is imperative that administrators constantly reflect on their own spirituality and beliefs and how they may be impacting the school's culture.

Expressions of Culture

Expressions of culture occur in many forms, but the most common are activities, behaviors, and communication. An effective administrator can lead these expressions of culture in a positive or negative way by example. Students and teachers will model communication and behavioral culture as they see it. Therefore, if a teacher is spoken to appropriately in front of students by an administrator, often he or she will do the same when speaking to others. Of course this is not always the case, but a positive atmosphere will breed positive culture and vice versa.

This positive atmosphere cannot be completed by one person's actions, but will become a slightly different culture gradually over time as groups of people and their actions work together. Therefore, students, staff, and the community have the ability to alter a school's culture with enough people's simultaneous actions. The administrator must be focused in order to maintain a positive culture by avoiding hostile situations and engaging in positive communications with involved parties.

Analysis of Culture

An administrator must always be aware of the culture in his or her situation, and constant analysis of the culture is needed. This can be done using the following phenomenological approach: describing, listening, reading, and observing.[17] First, an administrator must describe events and make conclusions about those events to see if they are leading to an overall positive culture. For example, an administrator may be present at a high school basketball game, and if the students are supporting their team in a good light, using appropriate language and gestures, then the administrator can determine that what he or she is seeing is describing the culture positively. Furthermore, that administrator can listen to conversations before, during, and after the game to see if there are emotional words of anger or frustration or happiness. Again, the administrator can make judgments about the cultural analysis of his or her school based on these comments. Likewise, the administrator can read documents, such as the basketball program, to gain insight into what aspects are important to the school regarding basketball, players, sports, academics, and so forth. If the documents show school support and spirit by listing players, band members at the game, school sponsors, and so forth, then the documents support a sense of community learning. Lastly, an administrator must observe all characteristics together and complete an overall picture of the culture in the school. Likewise, the administrator may need to initiate steps to alter or change the culture if a negative one exists. Change is slow, and an effective administrator will promote change at an appropriate rate with always promoting a positive school culture in the process.

Practical Discussions and Examples

The most important policies that an educational leader can have regarding culture are a respect policy and a no-tolerance policy. Often these go hand-in-hand. Students, teachers, and administrators in a school must respect each other. They do not have to agree with each other, but they must respect an individual's right to different opinions, religions, dress, cultures, habits, and so forth. By enforcing a no-tolerance policy, educators model that respect and expect it. Students will follow suit and show this respect, and hopefully begin to learn from these differences. For example, suppose that a small school consists mainly of African American and Caucasian students, most whom claim to be Christian. Beginning in September, two new female students who are Muslim attend the school, and they wear traditional headdresses or veils. During the first week, one girl in the school makes fun of one of the new students because of the veil. A crowd develops in the hallway as the girl continues to make degrading comments about her attire. Instantly, a teacher or administrator should intervene, reinforce the no-tolerance rule verbally to all those in attendance, and take the offending student to a private area for more discussion. Sometimes educational leaders and teachers are reluctant to get involved, hoping that students can work out disagreements themselves. Other times, educational leaders and teachers are afraid of bringing attention to the new dress and don't have the answers that they think their students will ask after intervening. An educational leader must explain his or her expectation that teachers stop any type of bullying right away. Teachers should take these opportunities as teaching moments about respect even if they don't know all the answers.

SUMMARY

This chapter began with an explanation about the rationale for spiritual leadership in a job setting where there are multiple demands on the educational leader. This model theory of leadership was explained as transcendental leadership. In explaining this theory, the following topics were described: spiritual leadership paradigm and elements; the reflection paradigm; the principal of subsidiarity; acts from a political base; acts from a sense of duty; one who advocates social justice; and one who formulates professional positions through discourse. The chapter ends with a discussion about culture—in particular the components of culture, the expressions of culture, and the analysis of culture. A strong educational leader is one who operationalizes each situation, makes decisions using the principal of subsidiarity and understanding of culture and duty, and then constantly reflects that the best decisions were made for those involved.

ILLUSTRATION: A CASE OF TRANSCENDENTAL LEADERSHIP

The Setting

Jamison is a traditional farming community in rural Kansas where the major crop is wheat. The town consists of a small downtown area with a few local shops including a grocery store, a hardware store, a dry cleaner, a JC Penney catalog store, a small clothing store, and a small nickel-and-dime store. In addition, the town has a small hospital where people go for minor treatment which has a helicopter pad to air lift those needing more advanced care to the next large town approximately sixty miles away. The town also has a small movie theater, a funeral home, two private lawyers, one pharmacy, one optometrist, a dentist, a John Deere store, and another farming store equipped with gardening and pesticide products. The "downtown" is the center of town where there is also a "square" with a courthouse in the middle. Homes are built around this downtown area as well as throughout the countryside.

The community has been a farming community since its establishment in 1899. The original settlers were German immigrants; therefore, the majority of the town is White and Protestant, with few other ethnicities or religions represented. The school district consists of one elementary school, one middle school, and one high school. The student population mirrors the town population. Therefore, most of the students are White, Protestant, and from a rural background. While some of the students would be considered poor, the majority would be considered low-middle class because of the lucrative farming industry in the last few years. Approximately 50% of the high school graduates go onto some type of higher education, although many do not complete their higher degrees.

Jamison High School is a relatively small high school with approximately 450 students in its four grades. Students live in the small town of Jamison (population 3,000) as well as up to a twenty-mile radius in the country area surrounding Jamison. The teachers in the school all hold bachelor degrees and teaching certificates with approximately 20% holding a master's degree. The average teaching salary is around $40,000, and many teachers stay in the school once hired. Most teachers live in the same small town or outlying areas. There is one administrator per building and one superintendent for the district. The superintendent's office is next to the principal's office in the high school.

The community consists of only Christian churches. There is one Roman Catholic Church and approximately nine Protestant churches. Some of the Protestant churches are nationally affiliated such as the Church of the Nazarene, the Methodist Church, and the Lutheran Church. Others are not quite as national but may have some affiliation with others like it in the region such as the Church of Christ or the local Christian Church. Nonetheless, there is a definite Christian feeling in the community where the majority of citizens belong to one of the churches. However, there are no religious schools in the area— only the public school is available for education.

The Situation

Mrs. Coleman is the principal of Jamison High School. Mrs. Coleman does attend church with some of her students and their families. However, she is aware that most of her students attend various churches in the area, or at least their families attend a church. The diversity in her school is not in which type of religion but instead in which "brand" of Christianity. The students in her school all feel connected to some church, but at varying levels. Some wear crosses every day on necklaces. Some talk about their church's youth group and invite their friends and other kids in the school to ice cream socials, youth group meetings, or outings to the movie theater. Others do not really mention church. And then others talk openly how religion and God should be allowed in public schools. Likewise, the churches in the town reflect what the students portray. Some are quietly religious while others are very vocal about what the schools do or do not allow.

Spirituality

Mrs. Coleman herself is a member of the Lutheran Church in Jamison. This would be considered one of the more conservative churches in the area. She sings in its choir regularly, and her husband helps with the church's bookkeeping records. While she considers herself religious, she would not necessarily discuss religion or her church at the high school. In particular, she does not discuss openly what she agrees or disagrees with regarding other churches in the community. Therefore, while she does not mind members of the community knowing what church she attends and that she is Christian, she feels it is in the best interest of her school to not pass judgment on other local churches. She would consider herself spiritual in that she felt education as a calling for her to help her small community. Because she grew up in the rural community herself and saw the value of education, she wanted to make sure that other children from similar backgrounds had the same access and opportunities to a good education as she did, despite their location or lack of resources when compared to others in more populous or affluent areas of the country.

The Problem

Each year the high school students vote on a theme for an all-school assembly. The theme is normally about a topic of interest and typically involves a special speaker or guest presentation that would not be a normal part of the curriculum or normal opportunity for the students. Examples of assemblies in the past have included a magician performance, a traveling theater production performance in the gymnasium, a local political representative discussing current political reform, and a past graduate who became an astronaut. This year, the students were presented with some affordable options, and the students voted on a popular "psychic" from the next larger town approximately sixty miles away. This psychic was not a television or radio star, but had been known for her work with the police in solving a few crimes.

As the date for the psychic neared, two particular Christian churches in the community began to verbally state their dissatisfaction with the school for allowing a psychic to "perform" on school grounds. At the time of the decision to bring the psychic to the school, it was unclear as to what exactly she would be doing except talk about her abilities and work with the police. Nonetheless, two ministers joined together with some members of their congregations to express their distaste with allowing any psychic on school grounds. It became unclear as to *why* they disapproved—it was either that psychics symbolized witchcraft which represented, traditionally, the work of the devil, or that it was unfair for a psychic, which to some is a form of religion, to be allowed on school grounds when their own Christian religion could not be discussed on school grounds. Both requested a meeting with Mrs. Coleman, and in the meeting, they demanded that the psychic assembly be cancelled.

Discernment Questions

1. What decision should Mrs. Coleman make, and why?

2. In what ways can spirituality affect the decision?

3. In what ways does the culture of the community affect the school?

4. Is the psychic an expression of the school and community culture?

5. Is this a problem in the separation of "church and state"? In what ways?

6. Should the psychic visit since a majority of the students voted for her?

7. Would open discussion about religion help in this case?

Conversations About the Case Study

Mrs. Coleman should grant the meeting, and in that meeting, she should first explain that the students voted for this presentation. She also should make it clear that any student who disagrees does not need to attend the assembly. However, she should also listen to the ministers' thoughts about psychics being a cult or type of religion. Because no other religion is allowed to profess faith in the school, then Mrs. Coleman must try to understand if the psychic represents a type of religion that should be banned from the assembly. Mrs. Coleman may also need to speak directly with the psychic to see what she says about religion herself. If she tells Mrs. Coleman that she sees visions that are from God, and that she is a special spiritual being, then it could be most appropriate to cancel the assembly if this is what her talk will center around. However, if Mrs. Coleman discovers that the psychic has visions but they are not related to religion, and she could focus her presentation on her detective and police work, then it could well be appropriate.

The Christian community surrounding this school obviously impacts both the students and culture in the school. One option would be to have an open forum about visions, allowing the psychic to speak along with other spiritual leaders. This type of forum may be best as optional or after school since the subject of religion will be discussed at length. However, the answers to the questions above really depend on the culture of the school and community. Every administrator must understand the culture to best serve the people in it. Mrs. Coleman must make a decision based on fact rather than emotions, and she must make a decision that is reflective and beneficial for the culture of the school and community.

EXERCISE:
CULTURAL ANALYSIS ASSESSMENT

After reading each situation, identify the feelings being expressed, the phenomenological dimension(s) of cultural analysis that the administrator must use: describing, listening, reading, and observing, and the appropriate response.

Situation 1

The principal sees an interaction between two of his teachers in the distance and wonders if anything is wrong because of the strange look on one of the teacher's faces. Later that day, he hears a rumor that one male teacher sexually harassed a female teacher verbally in the hallway.

Feelings: _____

_____

Cultural analysis dimension: _____

_____

Response: _____

_____

Situation 2

A bus driver reports that many of the students on her bus are acting up by shouting loudly to each other and calling each other names.

Feelings: _____

_____

Cultural analysis dimension: _____

_____

Response: _____

_____

Situation 3

A principal hears a teacher talking to a student in the hallway, trying to console the student because of family problems at home.

Feelings: _____

_____

Cultural analysis dimension: _____

_____

Response: _____

_____

Situation 4

A superintendent states in a faculty meeting that the board is not supporting her goals concerning improved student achievement.

Feelings: _____

_____

Cultural analysis dimension: _____

_____

Response: _____

_____

Situation 5

The board has decided to fire a new teacher because of incompetence. The principal finds out the same day as the teacher, and the school children seem upset at the situation.

Feelings: _____

_____

Cultural analysis dimension: _____

_____

Response: _____

_____

Situation 6

A principal wants to encourage teachers to use some money for professional development opportunities outside the school, and no one seems excited about doing this.

Feelings: _____

_____

Cultural analysis dimension: _____

_____

Response: _____

_____

Situation 7

An administrator learns that parents have been complaining about him directly to the superintendent about his leadership abilities in dealing with children with special needs in the school.

Feelings: _____

_____

Cultural analysis dimension: _____

_____

Response: _____

_____

Situation 8

A female vice-principal in a school has just learned that she was not selected for the opening of principal in the building for next year, and that the board has hired a male teacher from another school district.

Feelings: _____

_____

Cultural analysis dimension: _____

_____

Response: _____

APPENDIX A

Research in Astronomy, Geology, and Physics

I t is stating the obvious to assert that scientific advances are never in remission, but rather raging toward new and sometimes painful discoveries. Religion, either mainstream or otherwise, tends to react to every discovery with caution, lest our society loses sight of the larger picture. However, some of the relatively recent discoveries in the area of astronomy, geology, and physics have changed the way some people conceptualize the notion of spirituality. In addition, the advances in technology as an instrument in all areas of research have made available an enormous amount of data which begs to be utilized in the analysis of spirituality.

Paradigm Shift in Physics[1]

The scientific community continues to be involved in a paradigm shift that reaches deep into the very structure of certain theoretical constructs. The closed deterministic theories of Newtonian physics have given way to viewing nature as fluctuating. Further, the web-of-the-universe paradigm has bridged the classical fissure between different disciplines. Literature and chemistry were viewed as separate and unrelated fields of study. Now, it is easier to observe and understand the common bond that exists between all fields of study; the method and nuances of literature as a means of communicating concepts and ideas certainly affect the manner in which scientists develop and test theories. It is the symbolism of language which compels the scientist to construct hypotheses.

Perhaps the starting point of this new paradigm can be traced back to 1929 when Edwin Hubble, the astronomer, discovered that ours is not the only galaxy. Hubble observed that the universe is expanding as a consequence of the big bang which occurred approximately fifteen billion years ago. The laws of physics as they are understood today were inoperable at the instant of the big bang, which produced an environment of one hundred billion degrees centigrade. In 1963, Bell Laboratory physicists Arno Penzias and Robert Wilson detected a low sound and 3-kelvin background radiation, with a large microwave antenna which was a resonating echo of the big bang.

Obviously, the big bang was unique; it was like a bubble ballooning out and simultaneously occurring everywhere at once. The eminent physicist, Stephen W. Hawking, has stated that our galaxy is only one of a hundred thousand million that can be observed with powerful super-telescopes. Further, each galaxy contains some hundred thousand million stars. Carl Sagan tried to explain the magnitude of these numbers by suggesting that if the entire fifteen billion year life span of the universe were compressed into the span of a single day, the whole of recorded history would occur within ten seconds. Equally interesting is the speculation that there may have been more than one big bang and/or there may exist simultaneously with ours an infinite number of universes.

There are three things to consider when pondering the big bang theory. First is the rate at which the universe is expanding. If the rate of expansion immediately after the big bang fluctuated by even one part in a hundred thousand million, the universe would have collapsed before reaching its present form or would have ballooned out too rapidly for stars and planets to form. Thus, no life would have developed because the heavier elements required for life are formed in stars.

The second consideration concerns the four force fields (electromagnetism, gravity, the strong force binding atomic nuclei, and the weak force causing radioactive decay) that hold together everything in the expanding universe. If these forces had been ever so slightly different than they are now, this world would not have existed; hydrogen atoms would have dissolved into helium and thus, water and stars would not have been possible. There would be no supply of energy to sustain life. Further, no carbon would have formed inside stars and the stars would have remained too cool to explode as supernovas, thereby depriving the planets of the heavier elements necessary for life.

Finally, in the earlier development of the universe, if every proton has been matched by an antiproton, there would have been no world. However, for every billion antiparticles there were a billion and one particles which were just enough asymmetrical for the world to begin. Consequently, there is a precise calibration between the masses and charges of neutrons, protons, and electrons. Thus, the rate of expansion of the universe, the force fields, particle masses and charges became aligned from the beginning to make life possible.

Interconnectedness[2]

Once again, it must be remembered that Newtonian physics viewed nature as a vast machine which was invariant and repetitive. The concepts of ambiguity, contingency, and randomness had no place in the thinking of classical physicists. However, on the contemporary scene, matter is considered as bound or condensed energy which has been captured from the turbulence of the big bang. Matter is the stuff of all things: people, planets, rocks, and so forth. Further, matter is fundamentally indeterminate and is a potency waiting to be combined in unpredictable ways; thus, emerges the field of quantum mechanics. The Newtonian-established periodic table of chemical elements rest on an underworld that is less than certain. Matter appears to have the characteristics of both particle and wave. Also, at the subatomic level, atoms are entangled in everything else in the universe, and it is more appropriate to view matter as vibrating or oscillating rather than having well-defined boundaries. At the subatomic level, the entire universe is woven into humans and humans are woven into the universe—the one in the many and the many in the one.

Signaling[3]

Information physics, a carryover from quantum physics, is responsible for the development of transistors and integrated circuits, which are the essential components of computers. For Einstein, everything in the universe from planets to protons is a signal system; everything is a warp in space, which implies that everything is in process and never static. Soon after Einstein's development, others began to apply his theories to thermodynamics and conceived the proposition that over time kinetic energy (chemical, electrical, or heat) in all engagements must eventuate in waste and structural degeneration. As such, thermodynamic systems vary from their initial condition and, therefore, their futures are different from their pasts. According to the law of entropy, the future leads toward heat death which is commonly referred to as thermal equilibrium.

The new concepts of information, redundancy, and noise were developed in relation to thermodynamics and became a positive consequence of thermal equilibrium. These concepts allowed physicists to translate bits of information into mathematical terms. For example, an atom of hydrogen or the Crab Nebula in a time sequence sends outs signals in the process of constituting itself which vary according to a kind of redundancy. Physicists can decipher this redundancy through mathematical calculations which, in essence, serve as information or messages concerning the phenomenon under investigation.

From this perspective, nature is understood as an immensely complicated communication system that has been organized from the noise spewed forth from the big bang. Thus galaxies, planets, people, plants, and all of reality are viewed as open systems that constantly exchange energy and temporarily push upward against the entropic tide.

Chaos Theory[4]

Nonequilibrium thermodynamics or chaos theory studies nonlinear systems. The significance of studying nonlinear systems lies in the fact that such systems are extremely sensitive to initial conditions so that even minimal changes in initial stages of a dynamic process can create tremendous outcomes. Changes in the temperature of an ocean can produce extreme weather conditions that produce tornadoes, hurricanes, flooding, insect infestation, and other natural phenomenon.

It is significant to note that nonlinear, open systems are maintained against the pull of entropic decay by metabolizing chaotic, random energy. Thus, what is discarded as waste at one simpler level of organization is taken in and converted (as might occur in the formation of a galaxy) into more complex information/structure. There are two principles at work in such a phenomenon: (1) nonlinear open systems never produce energy in exactly the same form as it was received; and (2) the complexity of a system determines the amount of energy it recycles. Because human beings probably have the most porous boundaries, they are the most recycled entities in the universe. Thus, human beings are the most unstable and innovative. During each person's life span, he or she is continually dissolving and "re-enfleshing." The tissues in a person's stomach are renewed weekly; the liver is regenerated every six weeks; human beings regrow their entire physical bodies over time.

The implications from the paradigm shift in the sciences of astronomy and physics can easily be propelled into the fabric of other sciences because astronomy and physics not only formulate the agenda for the chemical, biological, and natural sciences but also deal with the ultimate scientific questions. Just as significant is the newfound license to enter into dialogue with the social sciences and with the humanities. The designations for the various disciplines are truly only mental constructs that were helpful in the past, but that now present an obstacle to a richer understanding of what it means to be human through a deeper understanding of the web-of-the-universe paradigm into which humanity is totally interwoven.

Geological and Fossil Research[5]

Geological research has clearly verified that the Earth is very ancient; being born between four and five billion years ago. There is also direct evidence that throughout Earth's history, geologic processes have unfolded slowly over enormous time periods. Further, throughout the Earth's development, life has been much diversified. At first, there were simple one-cell organisms living in the sea; only after a billion years did multiple-cell life begin; only after millions of additional years did animals emerge from the seas and inhabit the Earth; hundred of millions of year had to pass before mammals began to roam the Earth. The most awesome conclusion that can be drawn from the fossil evidence is that creation was a process; further, that creative process continues to occur and remains an ever-present phenomenon.

Another phenomenon has been revealed through geologic research that adds to the mystery of life's development. There have been sudden periods of carnage during which millions of species have been obliterated. It has been estimated that almost ninety-nine percent of all plant and animal life that ever existed has disappeared from the Earth.

The human phenomenon is a most recent event given the ancient history of the Earth. Although passing through many stages of development, animals that had human characteristics appeared on the scene approximately two million years ago, which was long before the oldest examples of human communication were chiseled, drawn, and painted on the walls of caves.

From the dazzling record of Earth's history, the following lessons can be gleaned: creation was and continues to be an ongoing process, and plants and animals continue to diversify in order to inhabit the ever-changing ecosystems.

Richard Swinburne, Nolloth Professor of Philosophy of Religion at Oxford University, is a well-known and respected philosopher who has written extensively about theodicy. The basis of his thought concerns the existence of God from a design perspective. His intention is to demonstrate that a series of inductive arguments have minimal impact when considered in isolation of each other, but when considered in the aggregate, present a case for intelligent design.[6]

Psychological, Philosophical, and Religious Approaches to Good and Evil in the Human Condition

Using the active imagination, consider a person who is the principal of an elementary school in a suburban school district who, because he or she is lonely, spends his or her weekends in singles' bars. He or she has had a number of unpleasant encounters with people he or she met at the bar. Even though the principal did nothing inappropriate, one of those people contacts members of the board of education and makes derogatory statements about the principal. There are literally hundreds of other stories that could be cited in this section which exemplify the human condition.

It was Sigmund Freud who introduced the concept of the unconscious not only to the academic community but also to people in general. All the unpleasant events and impulses in a person's life are not lost but rather stored in the unconscious. Freud conceived of two forces actively influencing each person: Eros and Thanatos. Eros is a creative force that inclines people toward beauty, love, self-dignity, and mature relationships. Thanatos is a destructive force that inclines people toward aggression, degradation, disjunction, fear, and hatred.

Carl Jung recognized a pattern to the images arising from the unconscious which he eventually believed to be universal although they are manifested in a slightly different way in each person. These are the archetypes which people encounter in their dreams, in their behavior, and in their active imagination. One of Jung's archetypes is the shadow, which is closely related to Freud's Thanatos and which is present in each person. The external manifestations of this archetype are brutality, prejudice, and violence. The shadow also contains great creativity to actualize each person's potentials. Because the shadow is an archetype, it is transpersonal in the sense that it is active in each person everywhere in the world. From his research, Jung concluded that real evil exists in people.

Also from his research through clinical practice, Jung postulated that there are many archetypes, another of which is the healer. This archetype is that force which can heal a person or save him or her from the effects of the shadow. It is a salvation which occurs internally.

Salvation is the act of saving someone from harm. Harm can be a physical, psychological, spiritual, or social evil. Of course, there are many subdivisions of these categories of harm, and more than one harm can be present at the same time. For example, a superintendent of schools can have cancer and be in the process of getting a divorce, which has lead him or her into questioning the existence of God and which has resulted in a state of deep depression.

Salvation comes to a person when he or she searches the innermost core of his or her being in order to reflect upon the meaning of his or her life at a given point in time. This reflection is usually initiated by some crisis but it can also arise out of purposeful meditation. This reflection can transform events into meaningful experiences.

Another dimension to salvation which touches the collective aspect of humanity in a dramatic way is emancipation. Reason became the standard in the pursuit of freedom from various forms of constraints. French philosophers such as Diderot, LaMettrie, d'Holbach, and Voltaire sought to liberate people from the fables, myths, and superstitions of the past. Emancipation meant the right to participate in public discourse and the right to create public policy.

Emancipation is a link in the chain that binds together all human beings and all human striving. It highlights the continual tension between rugged individualism and social necessity. The Enlightenment brought to the surface of human existence the conviction that through reason people could develop new practices which would give them ever greater freedom. Because of the Enlightenment, people recognized that institutional domination and coercive forms of government diminish their human dignity by treating them as objects to be used rather than as the subjects of their own lives. Throughout the history of this phenomenon, there was a conviction that the world is not a static reality but rather a work in progress that can be shaped and fashioned by both individuals and humanity as a whole.[7]

For people who profess a religious belief, the concepts of salvation and emancipation usually are not identical but rather complementary. While the Enlightenment brought about reform that was necessary for the betterment of humanity, nevertheless it did not produce a world free from discord and injustice. Further, the struggle to free the minds of people from superstition caused many to abandon their religions and to take up new myths.

Thus, emancipation is ongoing but in a direction which rectifies the extreme rationalism of the Enlightenment. It is correct to state that emancipation is a secular movement that attracts both religious and nonreligious people; salvation is an aspect of religion that can attract only religious people. To describe the religious dimension of emancipation, it is necessary to observe that people of faith may engage in the same type of activities as non-religious; they critically analyze the struggle of others, they establish a bond of solidarity with people in need, and they look beyond their own self-interests. The difference between the religious person who engages in these activities and the nonreligious person lies in the rationale for the engagement. There is otherworldliness in the intention of the religious person, which is to manifest the divine by transforming the world, and the divine empowers them. Religious people also have an advantage when a particular struggle fails because they can fall back on the divine as a source of consolation, healing, and hope.[8]

Practical Discussions and Examples

A leader must continually work to instill a sense of happiness, satisfaction, and empowerment in a school. Teachers and students must continually look for the good in situations where they are unhappy and continually grow and develop. A common goal of the general public school is to educate all children to their fullest potential while instilling problem-solving techniques that allow children to make good choices. This in turn would further promote strong future leaders of our country. On any given day in a school, students or teachers or administrators may be upset, worried, or saddened by a personal issue or something happening in the school. Too much harm for one individual can affect this ability to rise above and move forward in a positive manner. For example, a student whose grandmother just passed away and who has been struggling with personal relationships may retreat within himself or herself and become less willing to speak or work with others. This lack of interest in others is a first step away from a healthy, happy atmosphere. Many times, missing these types of signs or too much negative emotion at one time leads to suicide, which in turn affects harm to others. Therefore, a cycle can evolve if too many devastating things are occurring without intervention. Intervention that is often needed is first seen by a teacher or counselor. A strong leader is one who expects intervention and a hands-on approach from teachers and counselors. Teachers, leaders, and students must continually work hard at being helpful, compassionate, and positive towards each other in times of despair.

Mysticism

There is another kind of human experience which is not considered to be the product of the divine but rather a human phenomenon that makes it possible or conditions an individual's receptivity to the divine. William James called this phenomenon mysticism, which he sets forth in his book *The Varieties of Religious Experience*. Religious experience is always problematic because it is mostly a personal and private event and, thus, unobservable by others. Such experiences have been reported by a great variety of people, many of whom were courageous and credible individuals. These people and their experiences cannot be dismissed just because they were private occurrences. Virtually all religions have mystics who captivate the minds and imaginations of those who know them. Such is true even in contemporary times.

In addition to the issue of whether mystical experiences justify belief in a transcendental reality, there is the issue of whether a mystical experience verifies that the content of the experience has an existential or ontological reality outside the person. The position of William James was that mystical experience is self-authenticating for the person encountering the phenomenon. He considered the mystical experience as the most profound kind of religious experience. Further, James considered the mystical experience as transcending our sensory experience and held that it cannot be described through ordinary concepts and language. James also held that the mystical experience conveyed to a person the truth that there is a unity in all things and that this unity is spiritual and not material; as such, it is not something that the individual does but rather something that happens to a person.[9]

In most religions, there are common elements in regard to salvation. The most basic element concerns the goal of salvation which is usually understood to mean a radical transformation or transcendence of ordinary human life. A second element is a negative valuation of the human condition that is viewed as alienation from the divine because of evilness and suffering, which will eventually lead to death. This estrangement of the human from the divine can be rectified only through salvation. The origin of this estrangement varies; however, the beliefs can be categorized into two areas: the threat of death or the threat of life.

The threat of death is usually identified with the threat of evil. Thus, the mortal condition of human existence is associated with an ethical error made at the beginning of time. As a result of this error, humanity became alienated from the divine and seeks to be reunited with the divine through religious means. This tragic error also has inclined humanity toward evilness, which perpetuates the alienation from the divine. Thus, salvation is liberation from the necessary consequences of the primordial error that leads to life beyond death, the continued existence of the self in the form of an immortal soul or a transformation of this world into a state of perfection. Because of humanity's disposition toward evil, salvation requires the intervention of the divine. Christianity, theistic Hinduism, Islam, and Judaism share a religious belief along these lines.

Buddhism, Hinduism, and Jainism view the physical realm as entrapment of the spiritual self in gross or illusionary matter. Thus, salvation is liberation from life through the complete abandonment of the physical realm for existence in a purely cognitive state. For some believers, the ultimate goal is nonexistence. Human existence is understood as ignorance or as intellectual error, which binds the person to the suffering that is endemic in an unending cycle of rebirths. Ultimately, through knowledge humans may escape, be released, or transcend this world. Some people also believe that the release or transcendence will produce a return to a proper immaterial state of being or a full realization of the potential of the spiritual self.

Pursuing salvation may entail asceticism, ethical behavior, cultivation of noncognitive awareness, meditative techniques, the search for knowledge, and ritual devotion. The pursuit of salvation may bring about an improvement in this life and perhaps a cleansing or punishment before final transcendence. At the moment of transcendence, the person may be judged as being worthy or not of some eternal reward.

The question concerning the relationship of reason to faith in the divine has been discussed and written about since the Middle Ages. It is an important issue because reason and faith are integral dimensions of humanity that are continually lingering in the recesses of the human mind. Those who accept divine truths through faith would argue that what is imperfect bears a resemblance to what is perfect; thus, human reason has some likeness to what is revealed.

In a sense, reason has been utilized by believers in three basic ways. First, they use human reason as a preamble to faith by establishing that God exists and establishing the attributes predicated of God such as goodness, truth, oneness, and so forth. Second, they use human reason to illuminate revelation through analogies. Aristotle's concept of the soul and Plato's idea concerning the immortality of the soul continue to be integral to the tenets of faith concerning death and eternal life. Finally, believers use reason to oppose positions against faith by demonstrating that they are false or by demonstrating that they are not necessarily true. Some people hold the position that the world and humanity have always existed; however, for the believer, faith holds that God created the world and humanity from nothing.[10]

At this juncture it is important to distinguish between reason, faith, and theology. Theology is an academic discipline which studies data of faith and utilizes information and the techniques of other areas of human knowledge such as reason in order to gain expert understanding of what can be known about the divine. Faith is not capable of being demonstrated in itself as is the case with other areas of human knowledge and their techniques of which human reason is always a component.[11]

Practical Discussions and Examples

How does an administrator converse and deal with students, teachers, and parents concerning the concept of life after death? Again, an administrator will most likely have a personal, spiritual idea about this topic. The purpose should not be to instill his or her ideas onto others, but instead, to be informed with topics, such as those expressed in this section, in order to communicate with others in time of need. Suppose that a twelve-year-old student in the school dies from a congenital heart condition. The administrator will need to facilitate healing and discussion among the other students as well as the family. Suppose that the family is one who believes strongly in the will of God, and they believe that while they are sad at the death of their child, it was God's will and that it is for a reason beyond what they can comprehend. Furthermore, this family believes strongly in the eternal life and that their child is in the hands of God. A compassionate administrator may attend the funeral of the child, and most likely will at some point have a conversation with the family about that child. It would be helpful for the administrator, despite his or her personal beliefs, to have an understanding of the family's beliefs in order to offer appropriate condolences and speak with meaning to the family.

Furthermore, it is more than likely that the administrator will need to offer some resources for fellow students who may be facing a situation with death for the first time. As educators know, many young people feel they are immortal until something like this happens—it can affect the whole school. Therefore, while an administrator would be incorrect to console students by saying that the child is now with God, he or she could facilitate conversations where students talk about the afterlife and what they or their parents believe. Without promoting a religion, the administrator must be able to offer times for conversation to aid others in healing and understanding. What teachers and leaders will realize is that students are often better at conversing about spiritual questions than adults. As a leader, a person is not responsible for answering the questions but for helping students answer questions for themselves. Being educated about possible answers and supportive of differences, while maintaining a personal view of spirituality, will provide one with the tools needed to lead in times like those described above.

Endnotes

Chapter 1

1. Richard Grigg, *Theology as a Way of Thinking* (Atlanta, Georgia: Scholars Press, 1990), ix.

2. Mark D. W. Edington, "God: Amen. Discuss.," *Chronicle of Higher Education* LIII, no. 15, Section B (December 1, 2006): B16–B17.

3. Lilly Endowment, http://www.ptev.org.

4. Ronald W. Rebore, *A Human Relations Approach to the Practice of Educational Leadership* (Boston: Allyn & Bacon, 2003), 57–58.

5. Rebore, *A Human Relations Approach to the Practice of Educational Leadership*, 79–80.

6. Bernardino M. Bonansea, O.F.M., *God and Atheism: A Philosophical Approach to the Problem of God* (Washington, DC: The Catholic University of America Press, 1979), 82–83.

7. Frederick Copleston, S.J., *A History of Philosophy, Volume 2: Mediaeval Philosophy, Part I* (Garden City, New York: Doubleday Image Books, 1962), 183.

8. Bonansea, *God and Atheism*, 134.

9. Bonansea, *God and Atheism*, 361–367.

10. Scott Turner, "Why Can't We Discuss Intelligent Design?," *Chronicle of Higher Education* LIII, no. 20, Section B (January 12, 2007): 20.

11. Richard Monastersky, "Religion on the Brain: The Hard Science of Neurobiology Is Taking a Closer Look at the Ethereal World of the Spirit," *Chronicle of Higher Education* LII, no. 38 (May 26, 2006): A15–A19.

12. Barry L. Whitney, *What Are They Saying About God And Evil?* (New York: Paulist Press, 1989), 2.

13. Whitney, *What Are They Saying About God And Evil?*, 4–5.

14. Whitney, *What Are They Saying About God And Evil?*, 8, 11, 13–14.

15. Whitney, *What Are They Saying About God And Evil?*, 86, 87, 91.

Chapter 2

1. Ronald W. Rebore, *A Human Relations Approach to the Practice of Educational Leadership* (Boston: Allyn & Bacon, 2003), 3.

2. Gerald Corey, *Theory and Practice of Group Counseling,* 4th ed. (Pacific Grove, California: Brooks/Cole Publishing Company, 1995), 142–150.

3. Rebore, *A Human Relations Approach*, 7.

4. Rollo May, E. Angel, H. F. Ellenberger, eds., *Existence: A New Dimension in Psychiatry and Psychology* (New York: Basic Books Publishers, 1958), 41.

5. Carl Rogers, *On Becoming a Person* (Boston: Houghton Mifflin Publishers, 1961), 90–92, 194–195.

6. Rebore, *A Human Relations Approach,* 10.

7. A. Bandura, "A Regulations of Cognitive Processes through Perceived Self-efficacy," *Developmental Psychology* 25 (1989): 729–735.

8. A. Ellis and M. E. Bernard, eds., *Clinical Applications of Rational-emotive Therapy* (New York: Plenum Publishing, 1985), 1–30.

9. A. T. Beck, "A Cognitive Therapy: A 30 Year Retrospective," *American Psychologist* 46 (1991): 368–375.

10. W. Glasser, ed., *Control Theory in the Practice of Reality Therapy: Case Studies* (New York: Harper & Row Publishers, 1989), 5.

11. Rebore, *A Human Relations Approach,* 10.

12. Viktor E. Frankl, *Man's Search for Meaning: An Introduction to Logotherapy* (New York: A Touchstone Book, Simon & Schuster, Inc., 1984), 101–136.

13. Lucien Richard, O.M.I., *What Are They Saying About The Theology of Suffering* (New York: Paulist Press, 1992), 1–2, 110–115.

14. John W. Crossin, O.S.F.S., *What Are They Saying About Virtue?* (New York: Paulist Press, 1985), 58–64.

15. Lawrence Kohlberg, *Essays on Moral Development: The Philosophy of Moral Development*, Vol. 1 (New York: HarperCollins Publishers, Inc.), 409–412.

16. Ronald W. Rebore, *The Ethics of Educational Leadership* (Upper Saddle River, New Jersey: Merrill/Prentice Hall, 2001), 28, 30.

17. Bouchard, *Whatever Happened to Sin?* (Liguori, Missouri: Liguori Publications, 1996), 35, 56–61.

18. Rebore, *A Human Relations Approach*, 14–15.

Chapter 3

1. John C. Haughey, S.J, "The Three Conversions Embedded in Personal Calling," in *Revising the Idea of Vocation* (Washington, D.C.: Catholic University of America Press, 2004), 1–6.

2. Mary Elsbernd, "Listening fro a Life's Work: Contemporary Callings to Ministry," in *Revising the Idea of Vocation* (Washington, D.C.: Catholic University of America Press, 2004), 196–202.

3. Ronald W. Rebore and Angela L.E. Walmsley, *An Evidence-Based Approach to the Practice of Educational Leadership* (Boston: Allyn & Bacon, 2007), 81.

4. Steven E. Tozer, Paul C. Violas, and Guy Sense, *School and Society* (Boston: McGraw-Hill, 1998), 3.

5. Rebore and Walmsley, *An Evidence-Based Approach to the Practice of Educational Leadership*, 103.

Chapter 4

1. Ronald W. Rebore, *A Human Relations Approach to the Practice of Educational Leadership* (Boston: Allyn & Bacon, 2003), 75–78.

2. Carolyn Gratton, *The Art of Spiritual Guidance*: *A Contemporary Approach to Growing in the Spirit* (New York: The Crossroad Publishing Company, 1995), 2–3.

3. Diana L. Eck, "Challenged by a New Georeligious Reality: U.S. as a Hindu, Muslim, Buddhist, Confucian Nation," *In Trust* 8 (New Year 1997): 10–12.

4. Rebore, *A Human Relations Approach to the Practice of Educational Leadership*, 79–83.

5. Ibid., 79–80.

6. Ibid., 81.

7. Ibid., 82–83.

8. Frederich Copleston, *A History of Philosophy,* vol. 7 (Westminster, England: The Newman Press, 1963), 92, 95.

9. J. O. Urmson and Jonathan Rée, eds., *The Concise Encyclopedia of Western Philosophy and Philosophers* (Boston: Unwin Hyman Ltd., 1991), 23–24.

10. Marcus Aurelius Antoninus, *Meditations*, trans. Maxwell Staniforth (New York: Penguin Books, Inc., 1964), 1, 9–10.

11. Paul D. Travers and Ronald W. Rebore, *Foundations of Education: Becoming a Teacher*, 3rd ed. (Englewood Cliffs, New Jersey: Prentice Hall, Inc., 1995), 64.

12. Ronald W. Rebore, *The Ethics of Educational Leadership* (Upper Saddle River, New Jersey: Merrill/Prentice Hall, 2001), 227–238.

13. Jürgen Habermas, *Moral Consciousness and Communicative Action* (Cambridge, Massachusetts: The MIT Press, 1995), vii–iv, 18–20, 68, 86–94.

14. Jürgen Habermas, *Justification and Application: Remarks on Discourse Ethics* (Cambridge: The MIT Press, 1993), 150–151, 158–161, 171.

15. Myra P. Sadker and David M. Sadker, *Teachers, Schools, and Society.* (Boston: McGraw Hill, 2000), 168.

16. Ronald W. Rebore and Angela L.E. Walmsley, *An Evidence-Based Approach to the Practice of Educational Leadership* (Boston: Allyn & Bacon, 2007), 61.

17. Rebore, *A Human Relations Approach to the Practice of Educational Leadership*, 149.

Appendices

1. David S. Toolan, S.J., "At Home in the Cosmos: The Poetics of Matter=Energy," *America* 174 (1996): 8–10.

2. Toolan, "At Home in the Cosmos," 11.

3. Toolan, "At Home in the Cosmos," 12–14.

4. Toolan, "At Home in the Cosmos," 13, 14.

5. E. Kirsten Peters, "Upon this Rock: Fossils versus Creationists," *America* 173 (1995): 17, 18.

6. Louis P. Pojman, *Philosophy of Religion: An Anthology* (Belmont, California: Wadsworth Publishing Company, 1987), 38.

7. Denis Edwards, *What Are They Saying About Salvation?* (New York: Paulist Press, 1986), 255–276.

8. Edwards, *What Are They Saying About Salvation?*, 270–276.

9. Louis P. Pojman, *Philosophy of Religion: An Anthology*, 91–93.

10. Carole A. Myscofski, "Salvation in the World's Religions," *Chicago Studies* 22 (1983): 97–110.

11. Vernon J. Bourke, ed., *The Pocket Aquinas* (New York: Washington Square Press, 1960), 284.

Bibliography

Chapter 1

Art, Herwig. *Faith and Unbelief: Uncertainty and Atheism.*
    Collegeville: Liturgical Press, 1992.
Byers, David M. "Religion and Science: The Emerging Dialogue."
    America 174, no. 13 (1996): 8–15.
Dawkins, Richard. *The God Delusion.* New York: Houghton Mifflin,
    2006.
Fogarty, Philip. *Why Don't They Believe Us?* Dublin: Columba
    Press, 1993.
Hawking, Stephen W. *A Brief History of Time: From the Big Bang to
    Black Holes.* New York: Bantam Books, 1988.
Peters, E. Kirsten. "Upon this Rock: Fossils Versus Creationists."
    America 173, no. 16 (1995): 16–19.
Toolan, David S. "At Home in the Cosmos: The Poetics of
    Matter=Energy." *America* 174, no. 6 (1996): 8–14.

Chapter 2

Berman, Marshall. *All That Is Solid Melts Into the Air.* New York:
    Simon & Schuster, 1982.
Boadt, Lawrence. *Reading the Old Testament.* New York: Paulist
    Press, 1984.
Carmody, Denise Lardner, and John Tully Carmody. *Christianity:
    An Introduction.* Belmont, California: Wadsworth Publishing,
    1983.

Douglas, Mary, and Steven M. Tipton, eds. *Religion and America.* Boston: Beacon Press, 1983.

Gutierrez, Gustavo. *A Theology of Liberation.* New York: Orbis, 1973.

Hauerwas, Stanley. *Naming the Silences: God, Medicine and the Problem of Suffering.* Grand Rapids: William B. Eerdmans Publishing Co., 1990.

Nishitani, Keiji. *Religion and Nothingness.* Berkeley: University of California Press, 1982.

Stearns, Peter N., Stephen S. Gosch, Jay Pascal Anglin, and Erwin P. Grieshaber. *Documents in World History, Volume I: The Great Traditions: From Ancient Times to 1500.* New York: Harper Collins Publishers, 1988.

Toynbee, Arnold. *Mankind and Mother Earth.* New York: Oxford University Press, 1976.

Williams, John Alden. *Themes of Islamic Civilization.* Berkeley: University of California Press, 1982.

Chapter 3

Brown, Timothy, and Patricia Sullivan. *Setting Hearts on Fire: A Spirituality for Leaders.* New York: Alba House, 1997.

John C. Haughey, S.J, ed. *Revisiting the Idea of Vocation.* Washington, DC: Catholic University of America Press, 2004.

Lowney, Chris. *Heroic Leadership.* Chicago: Loyola Press, 2003.

MacIntyre, Alasdair. *After Virtue: A Study in Moral Theory.* Notre Dame, IN.: University of Notre Dame Press, 1981.

May, William F. *Beleaguered Rulers: The Public Obligation of the Professional.* London: Westminster John Knox Press, 2001.

Nouwen, Henri J. M. *Making All Things New: An Invitation to the Spiritual Life.* San Francisco: Harper San Francisco, 1981.

Novak, Michael. *The Spirit of Democratic Capitalism.* New York: Simon & Schuster, 1982.

Palmer, Parker J. *To Know as We Are Known.* San Francisco: Harper San Francisco, 1993.

Placher, William C., ed. *Callings: Twenty Centuries of Christian Wisdom on Vocation*. Grand Rapids, Michigan: Wm. B. Eerdmans Publishing Co., 2005

Chapter 4

Antoninus, Marcus Aurelius. *Meditations*. London, England: Penguin Book, Ltd., 1964.

Aristotle. *Nicomachean Ethics*. Translated by T. Irwin. Indianapolis, IN: Hackett Publishing Company, Inc., 1985.

Habermas, Jürgen. *Justification and Application: Remarks on Discourse Ethics*. Cambridge, Massachusetts: The MIT Press, 1993.

Habermas, Jürgen. *Moral Consciousness and Communicative Action*. Cambridge, Massachusetts: The MIT Press, 1990.

Jung, Carl Gustav. *Modern Man in Search of a Soul*. New York: Harcourt Brace Jovanovich Publishers, 1933.

Rawls, John. *A Theory of Justice*. Cambridge, Massachusetts: The Belknap Press of Harvard University Press, 1971.

Annotated Bibliography

Antoninus, Marcus Aurelius. *Meditations.* **London, England: Penguin Book, Ltd., 1964.**

While written over 1800 years ago, this work provides insight into both the everyday musings and philosophic observations of one of the great Stoic philosophers. This work, divided into 12 books of self-reflections, delves into man's search for spiritual awakening, ultimate truth, and virtue. In the Stoic tradition, Marcus Aurelius writes that a heightened level of spiritual awakening can be achieved through the use of reason over emotion and adherence to natural law. Modern readers should take care to contextually and historically interpret the language in this text, understanding that Marcus Aurelius's use of the word "passion" should be interpreted as emotional reaction without reason.

Dawkins, Richard. *The God Delusion.* **New York: Houghton Mifflin, 2006.**

This highly controversial book, authored by Richard Dawkins who holds the Charles Simonyi Chair for the Public Understanding of Science at Oxford University, examines the varying degrees of belief in God currently held by society. Dawkins argues how the belief in God practiced through a religious tradition results in social ills and violence. Dawkins utilizes historical, philosophical, and scientific texts and theories to augment the atheist argument. This book scrutinizes the epistemologies used to confirm an individual's belief in God including: religion, personal experience, psychology, neuro-cognitive factors, human morality, and spiritual or religious texts.

Glanz, Jeffrey. *What Every Principle Should Know About Ethical and Spiritual Leadership.* **Thousand Oaks, CA: Corwin Press, 2006.**

This handbook, part of a seven-book collection on educational leadership, includes questionnaires, self-reflection questions, and simulation activities in order to engage the reader in active participation. Glanz examines ethical best practices and how to resolve ethical dilemmas while maintaining an awareness of spirituality. Glanz also outlines five "essential virtues" necessary for administrators to effectively lead: courage, impartiality, empathy, ethics, and humility. This book is practice-oriented, providing numerous examples and approaches used by a spiritually aware administrator. This book was also written in alignment with the Educational Leadership Constituent Council (ELCC) standards.

Heschel, Abraham Joshua. *Man Is Not Alone: A Philosophy of Religion.* **New York: Harper Torchbooks, 1966.**

This deeply philosophical book examines the presence of God in the world and how people seek their higher power. Heschel, a celebrated Jewish philosopher and poet, attempts to explain both faith and spirituality using religious texts and personal experience and reflection. This book is organized using two main questions: how is the presence of God known (and how can humans encounter the divine); and how can God's presence be incorporated into life and subsequently, religion. This book, while utilizing Jewish texts, does not require an extensive knowledge of these texts to understand the book's message. This book has received praise from religious leaders of diverse faiths.

Houston, Paul, & Sokolow, Stephen L. *The Spiritual Dimension of Leadership.* **Thousand Oaks, CA: Corwin Press, 2006.**

This handbook, authored by two former superintendents and leaders in the field of education examines both theoretical and practical aspect of spirituality in education. This book is written primarily for administrators who are seeking to increase their effectiveness through the use of spirituality. Houston and Sokolow outline eight spiritual principles towards effective leadership: intention, attention, recognizing and developing unique gifts and talents, gratitude, understanding unique life lessons, utilizing a holistic perspective, openness, and trust. This book explains each principle using examples drawn from both the personal and professional lives of the authors.

Lowney, Chris. *Heroic Leadership.* **Chicago: Loyola Press, 2003.**

Lowney, a former Jesuit turned business executive, merges the Jesuit ideals into the business culture to produce best practices. Lowney outlines four principles through which to exercise leadership: self-awareness, ingenuity, love, and heroism. *Heroic Leadership* includes the history of the Jesuits and Jesuit education, along with brief biographical sketches of Jesuits who practiced the four principles with great success. Lowney describes the spiritual meditative exercises used by the Jesuits, but provides only a limited modification for those looking to incorporate these exercises into their daily lives. This book, while business-oriented, is a useful guide for educators and administrators seeking to integrate spirituality into their professions.

May, William F. *Beleaguered Rulers: The Public Obligations of the Professional.* **London: Westminster John Knox Press, 2001.**

May contends that professionals in today's money-driven, litigious, and tedious work environment often lose their sense of calling or vocation to their profession. This vocational fatigue results in the professionals' lack of recognition of power. As the professional loses sight of the power inherent in his or her actions, he or she drifts further from contributing to the public good. May cites eight professions as struggling to meet public obligations: medicine, law, engineering, corporate executive, politics, media professionals, ministers, and professors. This book examines both the personal characteristics and structural flaws which prevent professionals from engaging in best practices and service to the broader public.

Meacham, Jon. *The American Gospel.* **New York: Random House, 2006.**

Meacham, the managing editor of *Newsweek*, examines the intersection of religion and American politics from the founding of the United States through the Reagan era. Using historical accounts and texts, Meacham explores the religious and spiritual views of the founding fathers, and how these views have impacted both politics and society. This is a historically objective book, revealing the contexts and background of the founding fathers' views on spirituality and religion. The book offers the reader a balanced account of the history of the separation of church and state from Colonial times through the Civil Rights Movement and the modern era.

Nouwen, Henri J. M. *Making All Things New: An Invitation to the Spiritual Life.* **San Francisco: Harper San Francisco, 1981.**

This "small and simple" book, written in the Catholic tradition, is directed at those considering a life of spiritual or religious vocation. The author attempts to answer the questions that must be answered by each individual: what is spirituality, and how does one live a spiritually-rich life? Nouwen advises the reader to center the heart and wholly love the "Kingdom" to counteract the "worry"-filled life prevalent in society. The author highlights two aspects of life central to developing and living in spirituality: solitude and community. This brief book is useful as a simple tool for individuals to use in answering their own questions concerning spirituality and how to live the spiritual life.

Palmer, Parker J. *To Know as We Are Known.* **San Francisco: Harper San Francisco, 1993.**

This book, written from a Christian perspective, examines the quest for knowledge and the motivating forces of curiosity and control within the modern educational setting. Palmer explores the integration of spirituality into an educator's personal quest for knowledge and subsequent dispersal of this knowledge into the classroom. Palmer discusses the role of spirituality in teaching relationships, teaching methods, and what is taught. While philosophical, Palmer provides many examples of how spirituality can be integrated into the life of an educator and into the educator's professional practice by creating a classroom of openness, boundaries, and hospitality. While these broad recommendations may be useful, modern educators must also recognize the impact of the multicultural classroom and the individual needs and abilities of students.

Williams, John Alden. *Themes of Islamic Civilization.* **Berkeley: University of California Press, 1982.**

This edited book provides an in-depth examination of the history of Islam and the religious and spiritual practices which have evolved from the teachings of The Prophet. This book, using passages from the Qur'an, Constitution of Medina, Sharia, Haditha, and writings from Islamic scholars and Imams, analyzes the Islamic community, view of God, religious and cultural laws, the return of The Prophet, Jihad, and the practice of Islam in various parts of the world. The author intentionally does not address the practice of Islam in Southeast Asia in order to provide a relatively uniform picture of Islamic civilization. While printed over twenty-five years ago, this text is a strong, historical presentation of the Islamic religion and beliefs.

Index